By Harvey M. Beigel

PICTORIAL HISTORIES PUBLISHING CO.
Missoula, Montana

COPYRIGHT © 1983 HARVEY M. BEIGEL

All rights reserved. No part of this book
may be used or reprinted without written
permission of the publisher.

LIBRARY OF CONGRESS
CATALOG CARD NUMBER 83-80356

ISBN 0-933126-30-1

First Printing April 1983
Second Printing January 1984

Cover Photo: *Battle Fleet at rest with Long Beach in the background. Circa 1935.* LAMM

PICTORIAL HISTORIES PUBLISHING COMPANY
713 South Third West
Missoula, Montana 59801

CONTENTS

PAGE

PREFACE iv

CHAPTER ONE 1
San Pedro Becomes Battleship Anchorage of the Pacific Fleet

CHAPTER TWO 13
San Pedro Bay Operations

CHAPTER THREE 33
The Impact of the Manchurian Crisis

CHAPTER FOUR 39
The Fleet's Growing Impact on the Local Communities

CHAPTER FIVE 45
Naval Expansion and the Fight to Keep the Fleet in San Pedro

CHAPTER SIX 57
The Fleet Prepares for War

FOOTNOTES 70

APPENDIX 71

BIBLIOGRAPHY 72

INTRODUCTION

Every year thousands of people from all over the world visit the Arizona Memorial at Pearl Harbor, Hawaii, and sorrowfully read the list of names of the 1,102 sailors and marines who are now entombed in the sunken hulk of the battleship *Arizona*. While there is much the average tourist can read about the attack, little is mentioned in these accounts about the fleet before it was based at Pearl Harbor. The dramatic attack in December, 1941, and the excitement over the war that followed have tended to obscure the prewar history of the Pacific Fleet.

The battleships of the Pacific Fleet anchored at Pearl Harbor on Sunday morning, December 7, 1941, arrived there from the West Coast in May, 1940, for annual maneuvers. With the the international situation deteriorating in late May, 1940, President Franklin D. Roosevelt ordered the fleet to remain at Pearl Harbor as a deterrent against possible Japanese aggression. Before their sortie to Hawaii, the battleships of the Pacific Fleet were based 2,500 miles away at San Pedro Bay in Southern California.

ACKNOWLEDGEMENTS

I would like to thank the following individuals and organizations for their help in researching the naval history of San Pedro Bay, California, between the great wars. Without their valuable assistance, this book would not have been possible.

Clarence Bailey of San Pedro who served on both the *Pennsylvania* and the *Vestal* during the time covered in this book; Edward Hauk, Curator of the Los Angeles Maritime Museum, San Pedro; John Olguin, Co-Director of the Cabrillo Marine Museum, San Pedro; Long Beach Public Library; Long Beach Harbor Department; Los Angeles Public Library; Los Angeles Harbor Department; Pasadena Public Library; Long Beach Naval Station Post Library; and many old sailors and townspeople who so kindly gave me their reminiscences of the era covered in this book.

PHOTO CREDITS

CB	Clarence Bailey
DWHA	Delmar Watson Hollywood Archives
HVB	Harry von Bergen / Cabrillo Marine Museum
HMB	Harvey M. Beigel
LAHD	Los Angeles Harbor Department
LAMM	Los Angeles Maritime Museum
LBPL	Long Beach Public Library Collection
NA	National Archives
NHD	Naval Historical Division
ON	Our Navy Magazine
SP/LAPL	Security Pacific National Bank Photograph Collection - Los Angeles Public Library
SI	Southwest Instrument Collection
USNI	United States Naval Institute

PREFACE

Many residents of the San Pedro Bay area in California helped make this book possible. Representative of the many people the author interviewed were Clarence Bailey, a sailor based in San Pedro before the war and a lifetime resident of San Pedro, John Olguin.

Clarence Bailey served on both the battleship *Pennsylvania* and the repair ship *Vestal.* He remembers his excitement when he was ordered to report to the West Coast after completing "boot camp" in 1925 at Newport, Rhode Island. The thought of being sent to the Port of Los Angeles, a location not very far from Hollywood, the nation's movie and glamour capital, seemed to promise the adventure that the navy was famous for. Reporting first to the receiving ship *California,* Bailey and others were screened for their athletic prowress among other things and then ordered to different ships in port. Bailey was assigned to the *Pennsylvania* and soon sailed with the rest of the battlefleet on its "Great Cruise" to Australia and New Zealand that summer.

Bailey remembers San Pedro as the town from which sailors boarded the famous "Red Cars" for Los Angeles and Hollywood, just twenty miles away. Sailors, he recalled, also sought recreation in near-by Long Beach. As a "liberty town," Long Beach was not always a pleasant place to go. As in Newport, Bailey remembers that the men in blue were "snubbed" by "polite society" because the stereotypical image of the "drunken sailor" persisted. He recalls signs in both navy ports stating: "dogs and sailors keep off the grass." Much of the harassment of sailors ended after the navy came to the aid of Long Beach during the devastating earthquake of 1933.

Bailey and most other sailors seemed oblivious to America's approaching conflict with Japan. Bailey states "there was no animosity between the navies then and there were even occasional 'smokers' on each of the other's ships when Japanese training ships frequented West Coast ports."

Bailey later became a pattern maker aboard the San Pedro-based *Vestal.* Though the "battlewagon" remained the "queen" of the fleet, skilled seamen like Bailey felt as much pride about their jobs as any gunner's mate on a dreadnought. Among the only seventy-five pattern makers in the entire U.S. Fleet at that time, Bailey's craftsmanship along with that of other skilled artisans, played a greater role in determining the course of naval history in the Second World War than the general public may realize.

John Olguin's reminiscences offer a contrast to Mr. Bailey's. Olguin recollects the blue jackets when he sold newspapers along San Pedro's Beacon Street. As a young boy, he was impressed by the spirit and heartiness of the youthful navymen. "They were good-natured and looked healthy and strong."

He recalls that "everyone wanted to go on the ships with the big guns." On several occasions, he and other area youth were invited aboard the dreadnoughts for annual Christmas dinners served for local needy children. He remembers that the food was "rich and served with vigor." The navy let the young people have "all they could eat." After dinner, the crews passed out Christmas presents to the delighted guests. It was on a "battlewagon" that he received his first pair of roller skates.

Like many people in San Pedro, Olguin followed the athletic competitions between the ships at Trona Field. He recalls that "everyone fought to get to the top of the bleachers in order to see two games at once. When one football game got dull, you just turned and watched the other game."

He recalls swimming out to the *Medusa* and the *Relief* as they rested in the Outer Harbor. The nearby navy target rafts were a favorite place to sun oneself before returning to shore.

The navy at San Pedro in the interwar years brought back pleasant memories to Olguin and the "men of the fleet served as role models for many young boys looking toward adulthood."

CHAPTER ONE

San Pedro Becomes Battleship Anchorage of the Pacific Fleet

When tension arose in the Far East between the United States and Japan in 1919, the Wilson Administration transferred 200 warships to the Pacific. This powerful fleet included America's newest battleships. Admiral Hugh Rodman, commander of the fleet, brought his dreadnoughts through the Panama Canal in record time in the "war scare" atmosphere of 1919. The Port of San Diego was considered too shallow to handle the largest ships and so, on August 9, 1919, the fleet steamed north to what would become the new battleship anchorage, the Ports of San Pedro (Los Angeles Harbor) and Long Beach in San Pedro Bay, California.[1] Local patriots were ecstatic about the fleet's arrival. A verse in the hometown press exclaimed:

We are the hounds of the sea's estates,
We course our prey where the world's
ends meet,
We hold our watch at the western gates,
We are the great Pacific Fleet.[2]

There were a number of reasons why the San Pedro-Long Beach littoral was a suitable anchorage for the large ships of the Pacific Fleet. There was a 2.11 mile breakwater on the San Pedro side of the bay which created 600 to 700 acres of anchorage space, some of which was 40 feet deep. Operational conditions were reported to be near perfect with good weather prevailing 60 to 70 percent of the year. Admiral William V. Pratt, who for a time commanded battleships based at San Pedro, believed that the San Pedro-San Diego area was the best naval drill grounds on the Pacific Còast and that the fleet could not have completed its annual gunnery program anywhere else.[3] The ports of San Pedro and Long Beach also had good shop and repair facilities, were near off-shore island gunnery drill grounds, and had almost immediate access to the sea. Most important, Los Angeles Harbor was one of the world's great oil ports.[4] Savings in oil transportation costs alone went a long way in keeping the fleet within its modest peacetime budget.

Naval leaders were still not happy about the decision to base the larger units of the fleet at the San Pedro-Long Beach roadstead. They preferred a large operating base in San Francisco Bay or Puget Sound. However, Congress would not appropriate money for such endeavors, and operating conditions in San Francisco Bay at that time were very hazardous because of shoals. Fleet operations in Puget Sound were made difficult if not impossible because of the incessant fog and forest fire smoke.[5]

The Navy's main objection to basing the battleships at San Pedro and Long Beach was that the deep water area of the harbor was exposed to the open sea, and therefore subject to attack. While the Helm Report on naval shore bases on the Pacific Coast acknowledged the on-going construction of powerful harbor defenses at Point Fermin guarding the harbor, it nevertheless insisted that the anchorage grounds could easily be attacked by a "hostile fleet even though the risk to (that) fleet could be considerable."[6] While the defensive weakness of the San Pedro anchorage remained a sore point for some naval planners, that contention was seriously disputed by the Chief of Naval Operations, Admiral Robert Coontz, who argued that the fleet could remain there in time of war as well as peace.[7]

With the exception of a submarine base leased from the Los Angeles Harbor Department and closed down in 1923, shore facilities in the San Pedro area were nonexistent. At first, a slip near the navy landing was rented by the Commander of the Base Force for target repairs. When the space allotted proved inadequate, the target repair function was moved to the old collier, *Nanshun,* moored a hundred yards off of Cabrillo

Heavy gun emplacement at Fort MacArthur. Several large batteries guarded the port after America's entrance into World War I. SWI

USS Cheyenne (BM-10). Her twelve inch guns were LA Harbor's only protection before the Coast Artillery arrived at Fort MacArthur in 1918. USNI

Beach. In 1923, the *Procyon* became both the flag ship of the Base Force and the Battle Fleet's target repair ship. For eight years, the *Procyon* flew the two star flag of Commander Base Force on its truck.[8] One admiral who commanded the United States Fleet described his home port in the following way:

> *As for the battleship force, such a base! It was simply a large anchorage ground in the open sea, protected by a breakwater behind which three battleships, or four maximum, and a few auxiliaries could be anchored. The major part of the battleships were without protection. When at anchor they rolled more than they would ordinarily roll at sea. With no facilities for a base whatever, this delightful place was part of the Port of Los Angeles.*[9]

Yet San Pedro remained the major base of the battleships of the United States Fleet for the next twenty years. It was there that the warships rendezvoused, recuperated, took on supplies and had minor repairs alongside fleet repair ships. San Pedro was considered the battleship "base" of the U.S. Fleet even though no dock yard existed.

The San Pedro-Long Beach area would remain the home port of the powerful battleline of the United States Navy until it sailed for Pearl Harbor in 1940. Congress would not appropriate money for other West Coast ports that could handle the large warships and instead, spent all the available funds it had in modernizing the ships themselves. Between 1924-1931, thirteen battleships were modernized at a cost of about $6,000,000 each. Among the ships slated for modernization were the *New Mexico, Mississippi, Idaho, Pennsylvania, Arizona, Oklahoma,* and *Nevada.*[10] When the United States Fleet was divided between both coasts, the Battle Fleet was assigned to San Pedro. It included twelve of the newest, best-armed (some of the battleships had 16-inch rifles) and longest-ranged oil burning battleships in the world. With the coming of the carriers, *Lexington* and *Saratoga* in the late twenties and the heavy cruisers in 1932, San Pedro Bay was the site of one of the world's greatest concentrations of naval power.

San Pedro welcomes the Pacific Fleet on 9 August 1919. *LAHD*

Teddy Roosevelt's Great White Fleet as it appreared off Long Beach in 1908. Naval officers took note of the excellent anchorage grounds. LBPL

Destroyers moored in the Main Channel of San Pedro 9 August 1919. These ships accompanied the battleships to San Pedro, but would be based elsewhere. HVB

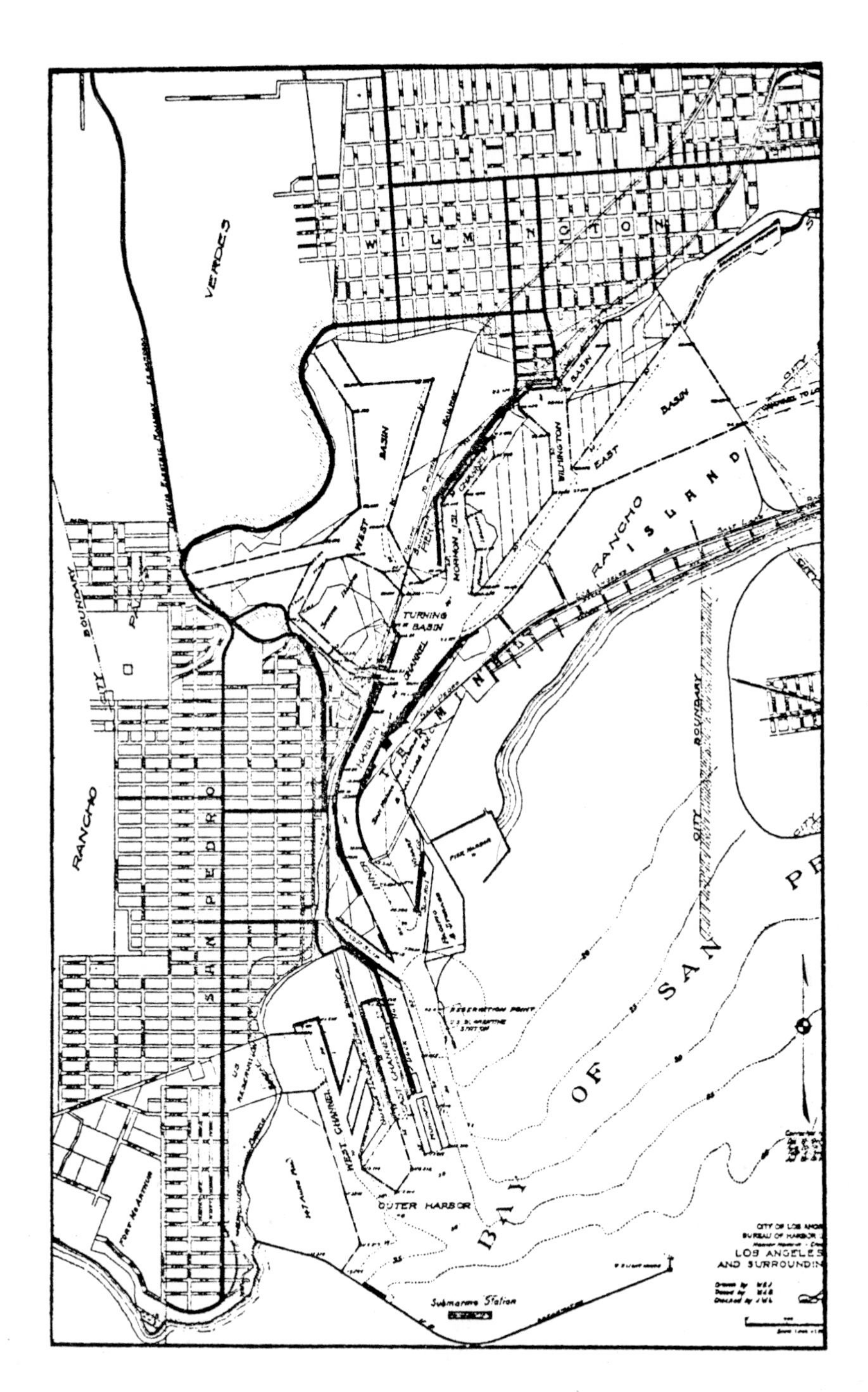

San Pedro area map from Helm Commission Report in Preliminary Report of Navy Yard Commission, 1916.

Destroyers in the main channel of San Pedro when the Pacific Fleet arrived in August 1919.
LAMM

Destroyers of the Pacific Fleet moored in the main channel of San Pedro shortly after their arrival in August 1919.
LAMM

Admiral Hugh Rodman's Pacific Fleet flagship, USS New Mexico (BB-44) upon her arrival at San Pedro in August 1919. LAMM

San Pedro Submarine Base. Before it closed down in 1923, it worked closely with the surface fleet in the harbor. LAHD

The submarine base at San Pedro. The officers and men of the base rendered great service to the Pacific Fleet when it arrived in August 1919. LAHD

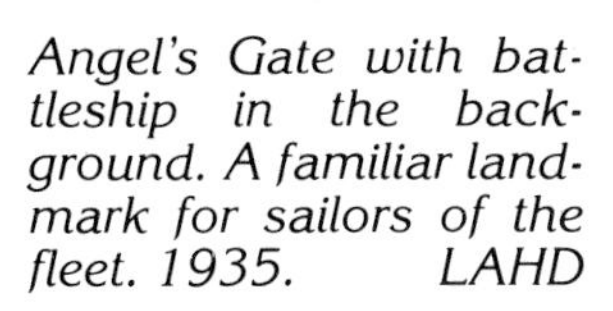

Angel's Gate with battleship in the background. A familiar landmark for sailors of the fleet. 1935. LAHD

Naval personnel in temporary quarters on East Channel berths during World War I. SWI

Naval Reserve Parade in San Pedro shortly after World War I ended. SWI

Visitors on board the USS Arkansas (BB-33) after the arrival of the Pacific Fleet in August 1919. LAMM

Calendar cover of US Naval Reserve Training Camp, San Pedro. The camp shared a warehouse with the Submarine Base at San Pedro. SWI

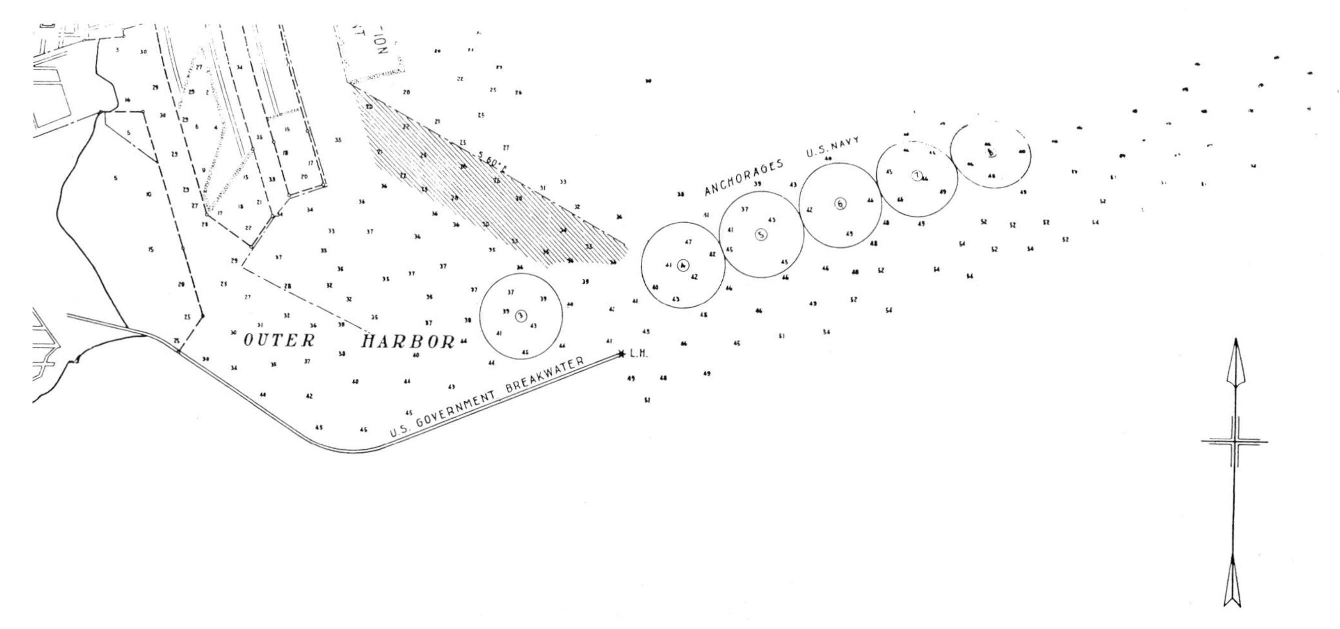

US Naval Anchorages in Los Angeles and Long Beach Harbors before the construction of the second breakwater which was completed in 1937.

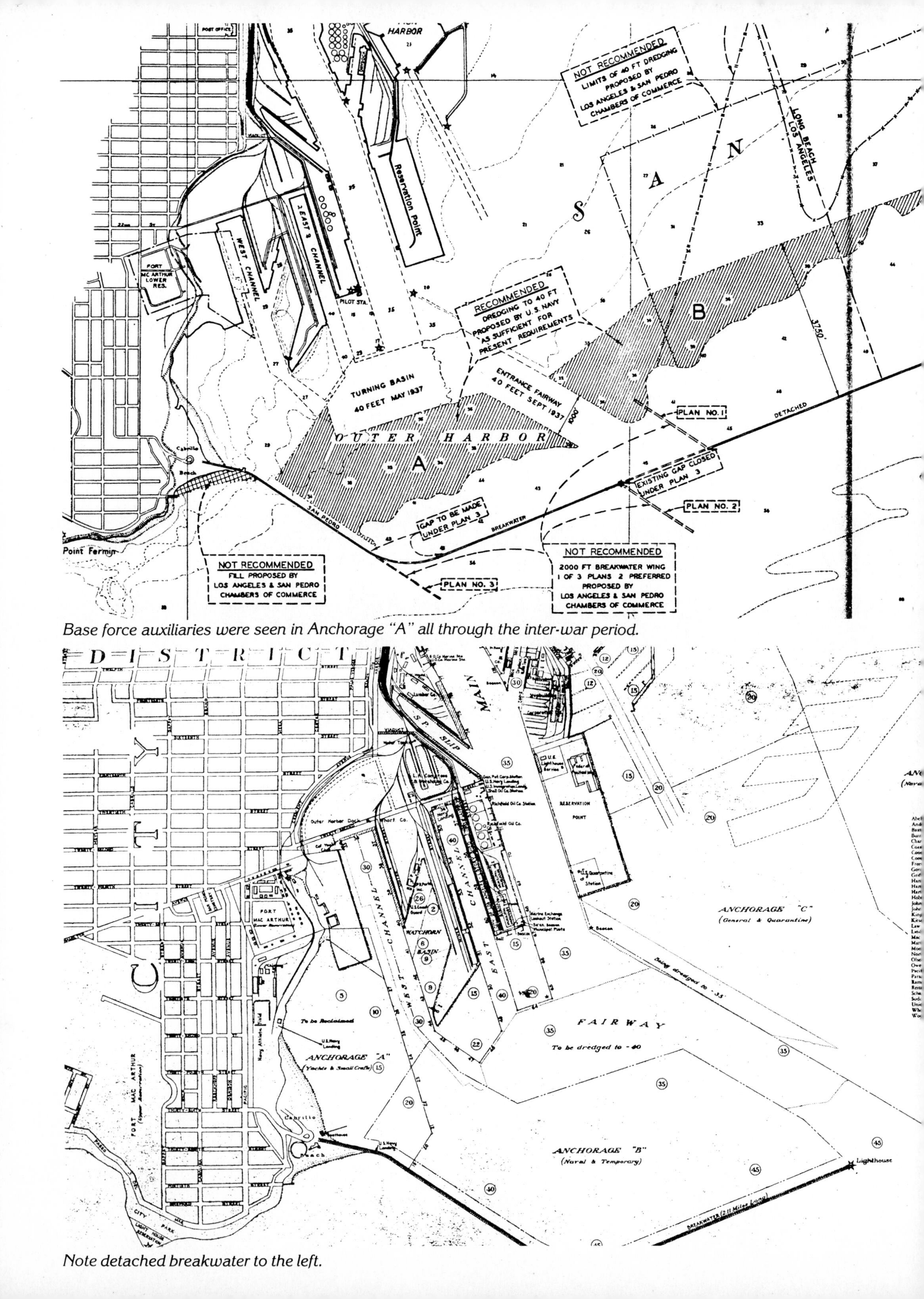

Base force auxiliaries were seen in Anchorage "A" all through the inter-war period.

Note detached breakwater to the left.

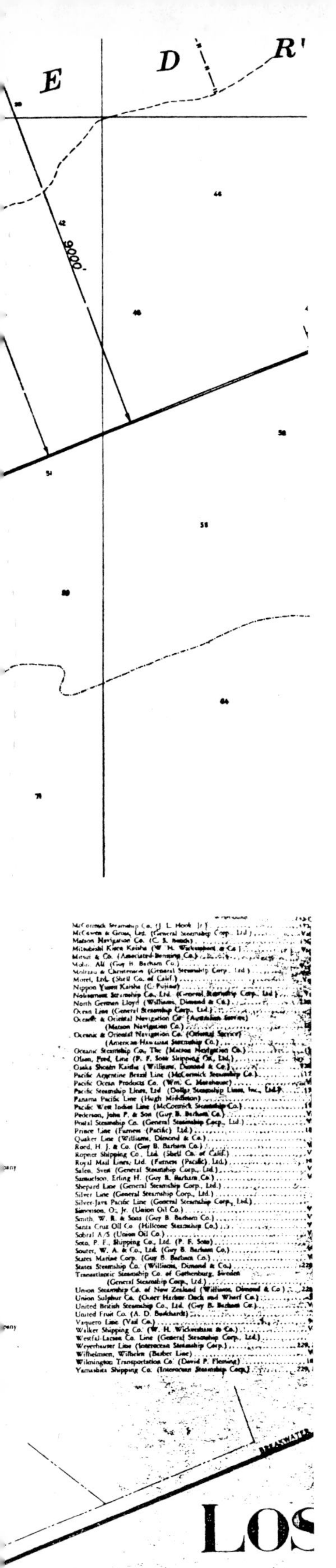

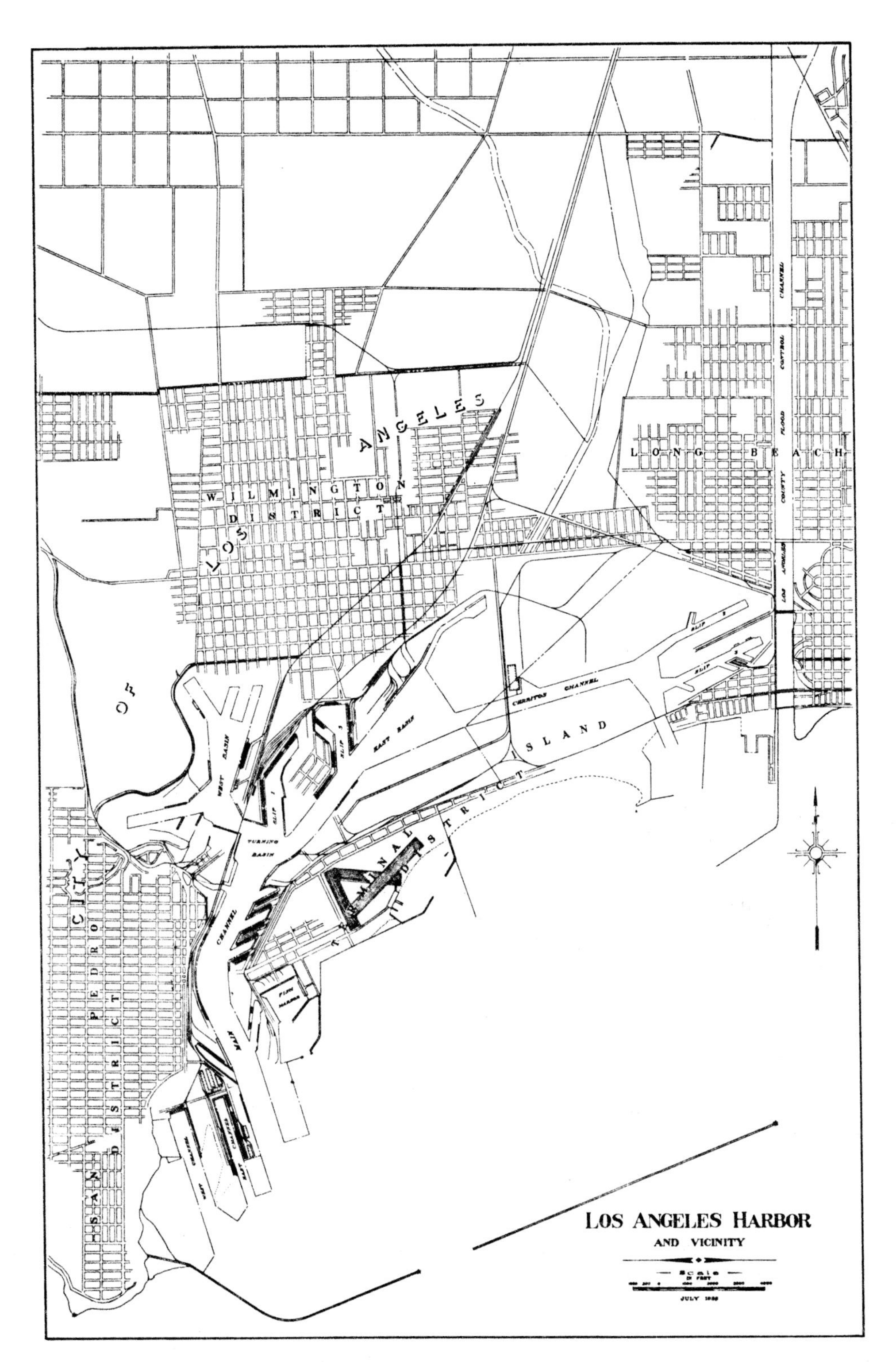

1939 map of Los Angeles Harbor which includes a view of the runway patterns of the Naval Air Base on Terminal Island.

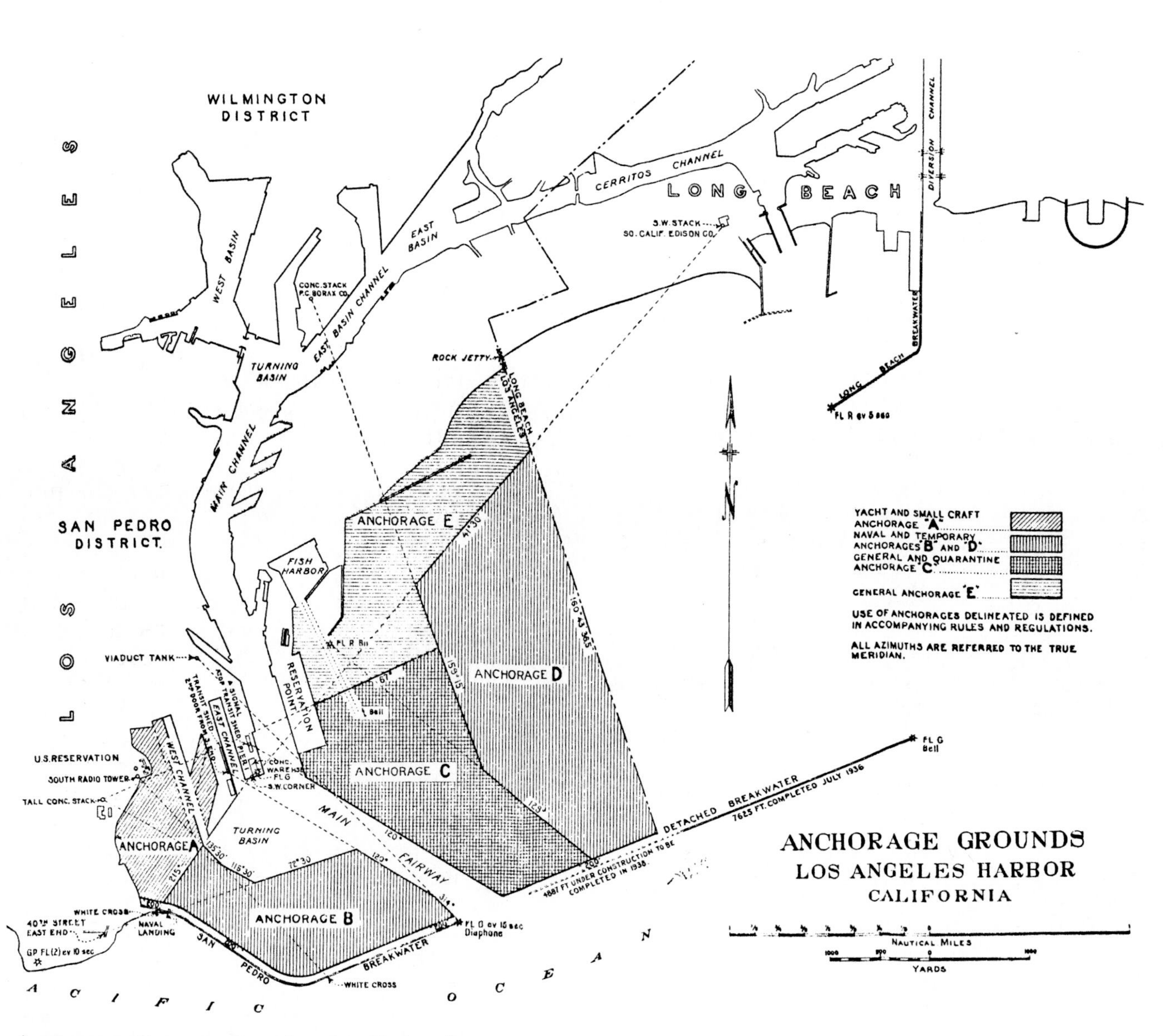

Anchorage Grounds, Los Angeles Harbor from War Department file, 1936.

CHAPTER TWO

San Pedro Bay Operations

The dramatic increase in commerce during the prosperous twenties brought overcrowding in the ports of San Pedro Bay. When the fleet was in port, perhaps as many as eight dreadnoughts anchored in the open sea beyond the breakwater. Because secondary anchorages inside the existing breakwater were reserved for auxiliaries, including a hospital ship, merchant captains were sometimes forced to anchor east of the battleships. The Port Manager received numerous complaints when surges ripped into the exposed ships and the port accordingly began to get a bad reputation. Moreover, the battleships to the east of the breakwater sometimes blocked the lighthouse, and some merchantmen were unable to get their bearings as they entered the fairway into the inner harbor. After discussions between the Port Manager and Admiral Edward W. Eberle, Commander of the Battle Fleet, the navy agreed to move one of its battleships and vacate an anchorage, and thus clear the entrance to the harbor for the increasingly heavy traffic.[1]

Overcrowding continued to be a problem as the volume of traffic into the port continued to grow. This was seen in the increasing amount of collisions between battleships and regular port traffic in 1928. On 17 March 1928, the outbound *SS Ruth Alexander* of the Admiral Line collided with the incoming dreadnought *Colorado.* The *Colorado,* inside the breakwater making its way to its assigned anchorage on the furthermost lee of the breakwater, got the worst of it. She received a hole on her side five feet across and ten feet deep. Luckily there was no damage below the waterline.[2] After a "quick fix" alongside the repair ship *Medusa* in the Outer Harbor, *Colorado* proceeded to Bremerton for more extensive repair work. The matter was settled when the navy and the shipping line agreed that the accident had occurred because of misunderstood signals. In a lesser misfortune, a Norwegian ship, the *SS Lei Langer,* rammed the *Maryland* as the battleship was returning from gunnery practice. The *Maryland* continued on to its regular mooring, but the Norwegian vessel needed two weeks of repair work.[3] As traffic increased and sheltered anchorages were at a premium, the increasing possibility of losing a ship or a command hung heavier over naval officers and merchant captains alike.

Southern California had a reputation for a mild, sunny climate, but certain winds called Santa Anas could be a tremendous nuisance for unprotected forces afloat. These winds brought 60 mile-an-hour gales, and even the largest battleships rolled and pitched, sometimes at angles of over thirty degrees on each side. Admiral Pratt remembered that sand brought by the winds was similar to an Argentine "stiff pampero" and cut into the paint of the dreadnoughts, giving them a "mud bath."[4] Frequently a second anchor had to be dropped to keep the vessels from dragging. Sailors were forced to use nets in order to embark on barges and gigs. Hearings before the Corps of Army Engineers for the purpose of building a breakwater extension were held, but government economies delayed construction until 1932. It was hoped that the breakwater extensions would provide more and safer anchorages and offer protection for new commercial ventures then under consideration. Meanwhile, the heavy ships of the Battle Fleet beyond the breakwater continued to roll and pitch until the completion of the new breakwater extension in late 1937.

In January 1933, an extremely violent gale hit San Pedro Bay. The terrific windstorm, caused by a freak atmospheric condition centering in an extremely high pressure area over western Nevada, caused much damage to many ships' boats, scattering them all over the beaches around the Outer Harbor. *West Virginia* lost a motor boat, a launch, and two racing cutters, while *Maryland, Colorado, Utah,* and the heavy cruiser *Northampton* all lost launches. Only three of the ships' boats could be salvaged.[5] As a result of this gale the navy began storing boats in the West Channel where they remained during target practice.

Probably the worst gale to hit the San Pedro-Long Beach roadstead area in the interwar period occurred on 24 September 1939 when fifty-foot seas and 60 mile-an-hour gales struck at a time when a massive concentration of 103 warships was readying for five days of extensive maneuvers. The storm's intensity was so great that the huge cap rocks on the recently built middle breakwater extension were lifted into the sea, allowing swift surges to threaten the moored warships.[6] Over 30 of the men-of-war put to sea immediately while other ships moved about aimlessly behind the breakwater. Rough seas prevented more than half of the crews from returning to their ships when liberty boat service was stopped. Thousands of sailors were forced to spend the night in Long Beach at Salvation Army barracks and libraries while movie houses and dance halls remained open all night. The damaged middle breakwater was credited with keeping the fleet from being driven ashore as it lay helpless in the face of the battering storm. The need to guarantee safe anchorages to naval forces prompted construction of a third extension to the breakwater which was finished during the Second World War.[7] Damage to fleet units was relatively light. The cruiser *Savannah* received a 26-foot gash in her bow plate when the storm carried her sideways against her anchor chain. The destroyer *Bagley* suffered similar bow damage while making a rescue attempt. *Savannah* was ordered to Mare Island for repairs; *Bagley* received needed repairs along side *Medusa* moored off Cabrillo Beach.[8]

It was during this interwar period that the San Pedro-Long Beach area became the major bedroom community for the crews of the Battle Fleet's larger units. Officers began buying houses in Long Beach in 1927 and by the end of the following decade, over 9,000 navy families lived in that community.[9]

But tight fuel budgets and unrealistic mandates from the Office of the Fleet Training forced the ships into operational patterns that frustrated attempts to ready the fleet for its mission. The training routine called for summer drills off Puget Sound and then a return to Southern California in the fall. During the year, there might be a concentration of the combined fleets off Panama in the winter and an occasional run to Pearl Harbor.[10] The core of the fleet training program, however, was spring gunnery practice off Santa Rosa and San Clemente Islands in April, May, and June. Devised by the Target Practice Office, gunnery exercises consisted of night practice, torpedo practice, and both divisional and fleet maneuvers.

Fleet at anchor viewed from San Pedro. Note commercial traffic and overcrowded conditions.
HVB

Fleet, train and target screens lie at rest in view from Cabrillo Beach in the mid-thirties. LAHD

Repair ships at work in the Outer Harbor of San Pedro. Officers had a convenient landing at Cabrillo Beach. SP/LAPL

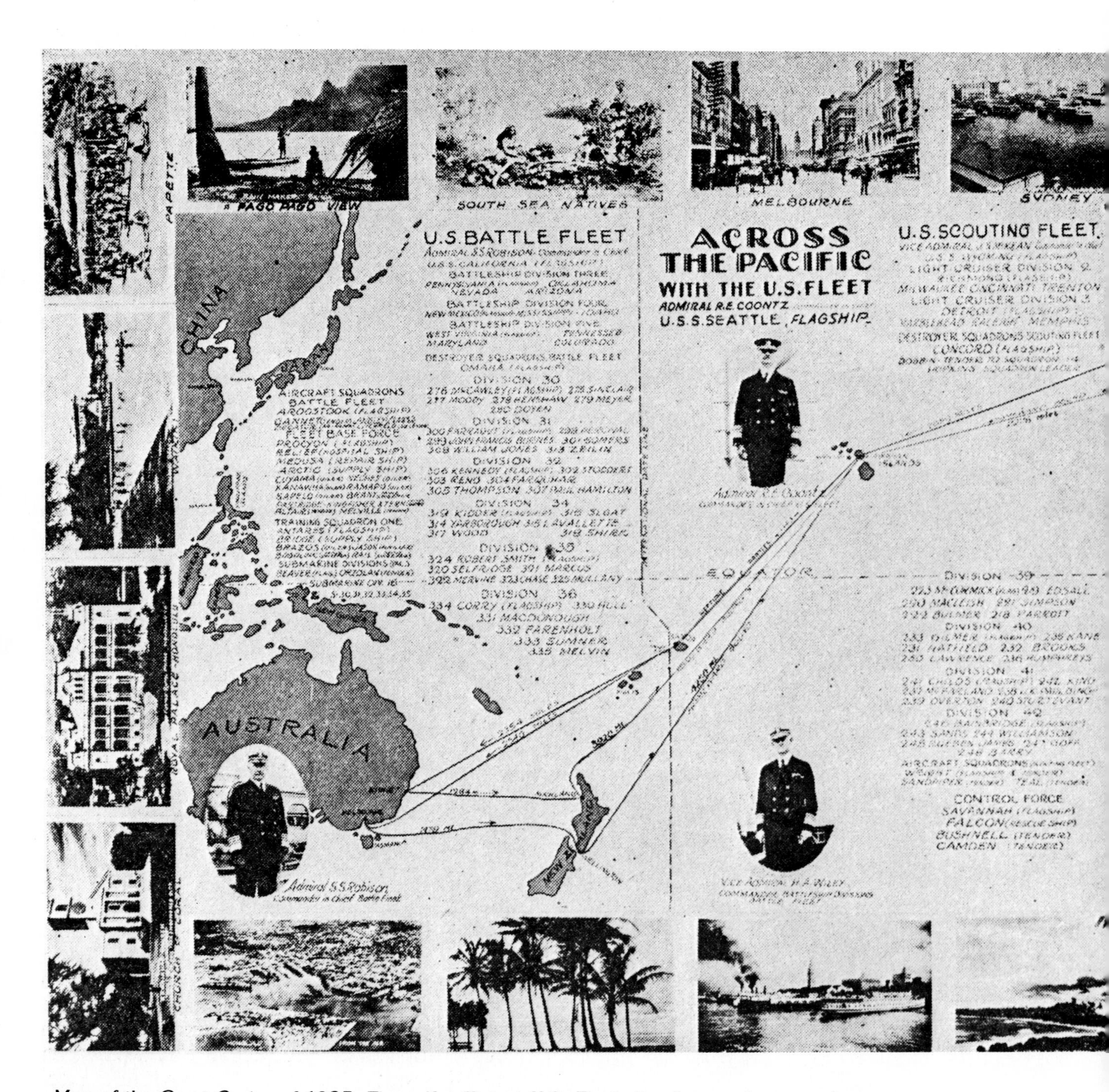

Map of the Great Cruise of 1925. The self-sufficient U.S. Fleet stirred anger in some Japanese quarters because the distance from Pearl Harbor to Australia approximated the same number of miles to Japan. HMB

These activities were competitive, and the ship with the best gunnery record won an efficiency pennant for the year.[11]

Particularly distasteful to veteran battleship commanders like John A. Wiley and William V. Pratt was the belief that domestic considerations and low fuel budgets dictated the course of fleet operations more than anything else. Wiley lamented that "men were seldom at sea overnight" and that many of them became accustomed to reporting to their ships each morning as if it were just a regular job.[12] Admiral Pratt, who commanded the Battle Fleet, was also bothered by the thought that the fleet's routine made an officer's career something akin to that of a shoe clerk or a shopkeeper. In order to change this situation, Pratt began keeping his battleships at sea for five consecutive days. With the slogan "Week out, Weekend in," Pratt found an excellent anchorage in twenty fathoms of water just south of Santa Rosa Island. Though crews were not happy about being at sea all week so close to home, operational results improved. In 1 January 1928, the battleship divisions fired their salvos in record time. Pratt also understood that week-out operations reduced the artificial strain that went with the rush to get home every evening after target practice.[13]

Local residents in Avalon, Palos Verdes Peninsula, and Redondo Beach, unappreciative of the nuances of fleet training, complained so vehemently about the practice firing that Pratt ordered his warships not to shoot within 30 miles of land, lest the charges shatter windows or cause earthquake-like shaking of dwellings. Complaints from Redondo Beach continued long after anger in the other communities subsided.[14]

Target practice was a very hazardous business. For example, the *California,* firing at targets towed by the *New Mexico,* almost fired on the ship itself when a spotter mistakenly placed the dreadnought's guns in the wrong direction. Fortunately, an alert gunnery officer saw the mistake and stopped the firing. In November 1931, an anti-aircraft gun exploded aboard the *Colorado* killing five sailors.[15] But the gunnery accident that had the most impact on the navy and local residents alike was the turret flare-up on the *Mississippi* in June, 1924, which killed 47 officers and men.[16] The accident was caused when 50 mile-an-hour winds blew down the 14-inch rifle tubes of the ship's number two turret and prevented the incandescent gases

Fleet on anchor on 27 March 1931 as viewed from Long Beach. Catalina Island is seen in the distance. Carriers Lexington, Saratoga and Langley are seen in the upper left hand corner. LBHD

from discharging. An explosion went off when the next charge was rammed into the open breech. Rescuers using acetylene torches cut through the heavy steel armor of the turret and found the dead gun pointer sitting at his post. When they tried to remove the body, the gunner's fingers jerked the trigger and the 14-inch gun roared its final shot. Fortunately, the gun was pointed out to sea.[17]

On 17 June 1924, burial services for the turret crew were held at Trona Field, the major site for fleet athletic competition in the San Pedro area. Officers, wearing full dress uniforms, and enlisted men from all the battleships formed a square around the coffins, which were almost hidden by flowers. Thousands of civilians, including the families of the dead men, listened to Admiral Pratt, the Commander of the *Mississippi's* Battleship Division Four, eulogize the men. Though some local clergymen protested that an admiral had no business officiating at burial rights, Pratt justified his role on the grounds that the men would have wanted to have a word from the "old man" more than from anybody else.[18]

Battleships in Outer Harbor, 28 March 1928. *SP/LAPL*

Battleship maneuvers off the coast of California, 1925. *HMB*

Los Angeles Harbor from Point Fermin & Long Beach, 15 December 1930. *SP/LAPL*

Battle Fleet steaming to the South Seas and Australia and New Zealand, 1925. *HMB*

Battle maneuvers off the coast of California using smoke screening. *SP/LAPL*

Inter-ship rivalry formed the basis of fleet athletic competition in most major sports. Boxing was particularly popular. CB

Program of

Group Championship Bouts
Battleship Divisions

on board

U. S. S. PENNSYLVANIA

San Pedro California

Thursday, 4 October, 1928

U. S. S. Arizona vs U. S. S. Pennsylvania

W. T. *Wortman*	J. W. *Greenslade*
Captain U. S. Navy	*Captain U. S. Navy*
Commanding Officer	*Commanding Officer*

Fleet athletics at Trona Field in mid-twenties. Battleship competition was fierce. SWI

Colorado shoreboats at the Fifth Street Landing on the main channel in San Pedro. Replaced by the 22nd Street Landing in 1933. LAHD

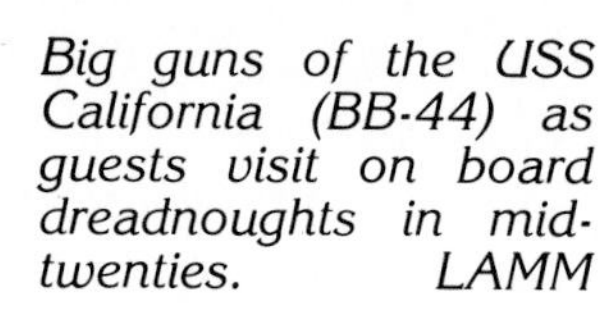

Big guns of the USS California (BB-44) as guests visit on board dreadnoughts in mid-twenties. LAMM

Navy Shoreboats, Fleet in background. SP/LAPL

To Their Memory

By Minna Irving

HE "Missy" is the proudest ship
That rides the billow's crest,
In gunnery she's unexcelled,
Her skippers are the best,
Five years she's held the "Iron Men"
For athletes none can beat,
And in efficiency but few
Approach her in the Fleet.

A greater pride is hers today
Though it is dimmed with tears,
For in her log a list of eight
And forty names appears—
Her seamen, unafraid, who met
Man's ancient grisly foe,
And passed with steadfast shining souls
To join the watch below.

Calm were the blue Pacific swells,
Clear was the azure sky,
Peace spread her wings above the world,
No enemy was nigh,
The Mississippi's mighty guns
At target practice roared,
When Death, a silent visitor,
Unbidden came aboard.

Through hatches battered down he went
In Turret No. 2,
Where round the giant guns they served
Stood all the gunners' crew,
Some thought of home and little ones
Beyond the ocean's rim,
Some thought of service-stripes to earn,
But no one thought of him.

Within that chamber wrought of steel
He grimly took command,
And turned its deadly forces loose
On that devoted band.
They saw him then—a dreadful shape,
They felt his scorching breath,
And knew him by his shroud of flame
And veil of smoke as Death.

They died as men in battle die,
Each sailor at his post,
Fit mates of Lawrence, Hull, Paul Jones,
And all that hero host,
With Skrynas at the telephone
His last report to give,
While Ensign Erwin stepped aside
That other lads might live.

Horatius at the bridge, El Cid,
Great Charlemagne of old,
Rustem the peerless Persian—they
Were men of god-like mold,
The crew of Turret No. 2,
Who perished at their guns,
When Glory calls the roll reply
With these illustrious ones.

Oh! it is not her battleships
That makes the Navy strong.
The thickness of her armor-plates,
Her batteries in song,
Her might is in her sturdy tars
To flag and service true,
Like those immortal men who died
In Turret No. 2.

Poem to the memory of the crew of gun turret number 2. ON

USS Mississippi (BB-41) was the winner of many gunnery awards. She lost 47 men in a turret flare-up in 1924. Commanded later by Captain Raymond A. Spruance, the "Missy" missed the Pearl Harbor tragedy when she was transferred to the Atlantic in 1941. USNI

Funeral services for the gun crew aboard the USS Mississippi that perished in a gun flareup. Note large numbers of civilians in the bleachers. LBPL

Funeral services for the victims of the gun flareup aboard the USS Mississippi. Held on 17 June 1924 at Trona Field in San Pedro. SWI

String of U.S. ships with Maryland class battleship on the right. SP/LAPL

USS Connecticut (BB-18) when it was Flagship of the Pacific Train, October 1921-22. LAHD

USS Texas (BB-35). For a time this battleship was the flagship of the United States Fleet and Battleship Div. 1. She spent more time, however, on the East Coast during the inter-war period. USNI

USS New Mexico (BB-40) before her 1931-33 conversion. She became the flagship of the newly organized Pacific Fleet in 1919. Point Fermin is in the background. USNI

USS West Virginia (BB-48) became the flagship for the Commander, Battleship Divisions, Battle Fleet, on 30 October 1924. USNI

A public water taxi hurrying by the USS Arizona (BB-39) in 1937. SP/LAPL

USS Arizona (BB-39) being refueled by USS Cuyama (AO-3) in the San Pedro-Long Beach roadstead, circa 1935. SP/LAPL

USS Pennsylvania (BB-39) anchored west of Long Beach circa 1935. SP/LAPL

USS Seattle (CA-11) was flagship for Commander-in-Chief of the United States Fleet, between 1923 and 1927. She was flagship of the fleet during the Cruise to Australia and New Zealand in 1925. USNI

USS Connecticut was assigned as flagship of the Pacific Train arriving in San Pedro on 28 October 1921. She was decommissioned in the Spring of 1923. LAMM

USS Procyon (AG-11) served for years as flagship of Commander Fleet Base Force, U.S. Battle fleet until decommissioned on 1 April 1931. USNI

The Hospital Ship USS Mercy (AH-4) in San Pedro, 30 September 1920. LAHD

USS Relief (AH-1) This hospital ship made its home in San Pedro's Outer Harbor. It was reported in 1926 that a wounded sea lion climbed up the gang plank of this ship, selecting it over other ships at anchor. NA

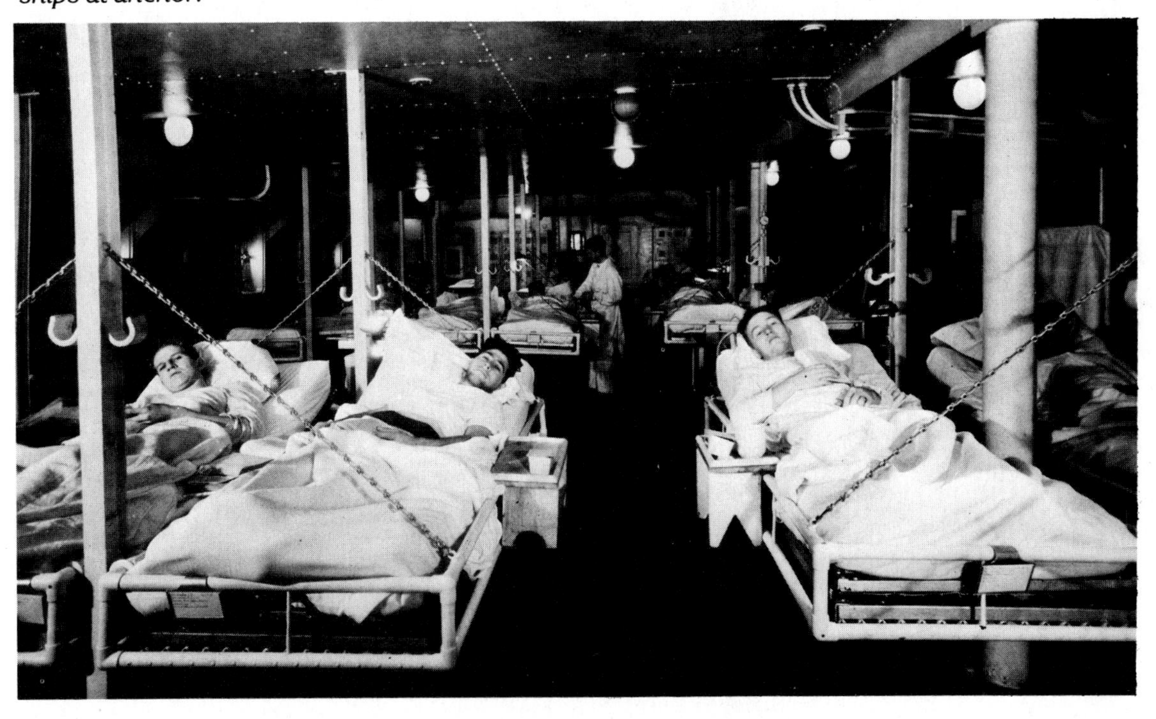

Men in the surgical wards received the best care. The USS Relief could handle 360 cases, more than the average hospital without crowding. SP/LAPL

USS Vestal (AR-4). This repair ship served the Battle Fleet almost uninterruptedly from 1927 to 1940 when she followed the fleet to Pearl Harbor. NA

USS Medusa (AR-1) was designed as a repair ship for major repairs beyond a fighting ships own capacity, but without benefit of a Navy Yard. Served in Train Squadron 2 in San Pedro from 1924 until the fleet sortied to Pearl Harbor in 1940. NA

CHAPTER THREE

The Impact of the Manchurian Crisis

Admiral Pratt had gone up the navy's promotional ladder and was Chief of Naval Operations (CNO) when Japan, in defiance of the Open Door Policy and the Pact of Paris of 1927, attacked the Chinese province of Manchuria in September 1931. Having been recently Commander, Battleship Divisions of the Battle Force, Pratt knew better than anyone else the weakened state of fleet readiness, and shuddered at the logistical problems involved in positioning the fleet in the western Pacific. Angered further by Japan's assault on Shanghai in January 1932, Secretary of State Henry Stimson wanted to bluff the Japanese War Lords by ordering the fleet, then conducting war games off Hawaii, to remain in that area.[1] He hoped that this act would stabilize conditions in the western Pacific. But Pearl Harbor, as Pratt and others knew, could not handle the entire fleet. The harbor was in need of further dredging. The battleships, moreover, would have to unload their fuel and ammunition to successfully berth there.[2] The vulnerability of Pearl Harbor to a sneak-attack was also well known. In recent war games, Admiral Harry E. Yarnell had led a successful strike on the island of Oahu.

Stimson and Pratt decided to do the next best things to demonstrate America's disapproval of Japanese actions. Heavy cruisers of the East Coast-based Scouting Force, on joint maneuvers with the battleship divisions of the U.S. Fleet, were ordered in early 1932 to remain on the Pacific Coast. These warships would be "temporarily" based in the San Pedro-Long Beach roadstead.[3] When Japanese Ambassador to the United States, Katsuji Debuchi, protested to the State Department about stationing so many ships on the Pacific Coast, Stimson answered that the American action seemed obvious and necessary. And when later pressed for a return of the Scouting Force to its East Coast yards, Stimson, mindful that the combined American fleets were greater than any Japanese force, reiterated that the "Pacific is now the most appropriate place for it to be," and that its presence would have a wholesome effect upon the sentiment of both the Japanese military and the Japanese people.[4]

In mid-April 1932, at the height of the Far Eastern crisis, one of the most impressive displays of American naval strength since the First World War took place off the San Pedro-Long Beach roadstead. Over 120 American warships demonstrated their power with a naval review that extended from Point Fermin to Malibu. The men-of-war, including 24 ships of the Scouting Force, paraded in an area twelve miles in length, three miles from the shoreline. They would move up the coast and remain in San Francisco for a month. Widely advertised throughout the area, it was estimated that over 250,000 people witnessed the demonstration from the Point Fermin-Redondo Beach area alone.[5] Though the ostensible occasion for the review was the celebration of Flag Day, there is no doubt that the most-hoped-for spectator would be the Empire of Japan.

Witnessing the review off Point Fermin was Admiral William H. Standley, the former Commander, Cruisers Scouting Force (Crudivscofor), now the newly appointed Chief of Naval Operations (CNO). Standley later told President Franklin D. Roosevelt that while the Point Fermin review was a "most impressive sight," he felt it was "a gross deception of the American people." The "glistening grey ships coming out of the white fog," according to the Admiral, was a "phantom fleet." The battle efficiency of the fleet, Standley believed, was extremely poor because of manpower shortages, and he was convinced that most of the ships could not maintain full power for more than four hours. Standley told the president that the fleet was

Aerial View of the Navy Landing at Long Beach in September, 1938. The two cruisers in the upper-center are the flagships of the Scouting Force and Cruiser Divisions. The rest of the cruisers were farther out in the Bay behind the battleships. LBHD

30,000 men short to be an effective fighting force.[6] If Japan were also aware of what Admiral Standley knew, the massive naval demonstration would hardly impress the military and political leaders of the island empire. In stark contrast with Standley's view was Captain Ernest J. King's contention that his carrier, the *Lexington,* "was ready to go into battle" during the Manchurian crisis. Leaving its home port of Long Beach, the *Lexington* sailed to San Francisco where under tight security it loaded planes and ammunition and sped toward Hawaii. When the crisis subsided the carrier returned, but according to King the *Lexington* had been ready.[7]

Admiral William V. Pratt on the left with Vice Admiral L.M. Nulton. Pratt as Chief of Naval Operations (CNO) ordered the heavy cruisers of the Scouting Force to remain on the West Coast in 1932. HMB

Crowds at the San Pedro Navy Landing waiting to get a glimpse of the USS Constitution on 27 October 1933. LAHD

The USS Constitution at Pier 57 on 27 October 1933. The ship also visited Long Beach. LAHD

Increased interest in the Navy was expressed when large crowds visited the USS Constitution at San Pedro's Berth 57. Accompanying the venerable ship are the Omaha (CL-4), the destroyer High and the submarine Dolphin. LAHD

USS Chicago (CA-29) was flagship of the Commander Cruisers, Scouting Force when East Coast based cruisers were tranferred to the Pacific after the Japanese invasion of Manchuria. USNI

USS Indiananpolis (CA-35) was the Flagship of the Scouting Force when the Force's home port was changed to San Pedro in the Fall of 1934. USNI

From the Tokyo Asahi, May 12.

"NEW MONSTERS ON THE PACIFIC OCEAN"

The American fleet and airplanes are operating in the Pacific.

From the Yomiuri, May 12.

"THE GREAT AMERICAN CIRCUS OF 450 AIRPLANES"

The circus manager is crying aloud for the great show, while Japanese children are gathered in front of the Japan-Manchoukuo-Chinese shop.

Japanese Press accounts of American naval maneuvers in the northern Pacific. The Fleet Problem began on 29 April 1934.

Despite growing tensions between the United States and Japan, regular visits by Japanese training ships continued. IJN Yakumo tied up at a berth in San Pedro's East Channel 15 July 1936.
LAHD

CHAPTER FOUR

The Fleet's Growing Impact on the Local Communities

Business men and merchants in the San Pedro area were grateful when units of the Atlantic-based Scouting Force remained in the San Pedro area for an indefininte stay. They were gratified when official orders in the Fall of 1934 changed the home port of the Scouting Force from New York to San-Pedro.[1] It was felt that the added influx of naval personnel and their families might be the shot-in-the-arm to the depression-ridden local economy. By 1934, the fleet based in the harbor area had swelled to 16 battleships and carriers, 14 cruisers, and 16 support ships manned by a total of 31,286 officers and men.[2] After the passage of the Vinson-Trammel Navy Bill in 1934 authorizing the eventual building of 102 new vessels, the number of ships increased significantly as most of the navy's new construction was ordered to the Pacific.[3]

Under these circumstances, the Navy would play a growing role in the economy of the two ports. Business activity would be stimulated with money spent by naval personnel and their families and local purchases made for fleet operations. One local newspaper claimed that 75% of the $2,800,000 monthly payroll was spent in Long Beach where 900 officers and 1,879 enlisted men made their homes. Indeed the newspaper continued: "The Navy is this city's largest industry."[4] In late 1932 the City spent $15,000 for a new navy landing and $10,000 for an athletic field. Smaller San Pedro also benefitted from the presence of the fleet despite the fact that eight out of every ten shore boats headed for the Navy Landing at Long Beach and not San Pedro.[5] In July 1932, 260 naval officers and 1,600 enlisted men made their homes in the San Pedro area. When queried by a local journalist on what the navy's yearly expenditures at the twin ports were, the then Commander-in-Chief of the United States Fleet Admiral Joseph M. Reeves, responded in round numbers. He estimated that $21,000,000 was paid out in payrolls and $2,150,000 was given out in subsistence costs. Oil and gasoline expenses were $2,130,000 while maintenance supplies and equipment purchases were $670,000 and $460,000 a year respectively for a total of $26,410,000 a year.[6] One battleship alone, the *Colorado,* reported that pay and subsistence figures for 1933 were $1,307,217.42, while the fuel, maintenance and supply bill was $1,406,324.97. Over $100,000 a month was remitted to the dreadnought's crew in pay and subsistence benefits. The average pay per man, including officers and enlisted men, was around $1,200 compared with $1,500 a year paid to the average worker in industry.[7]

Business was brisk in San Pedro and Long Beach despite the general depression in many adjacent communities. In Long Beach one jewelry store had over 2,000 navy accounts, selling a large number of watches, a popular gift for sailors' girl friends. A Long Beach car dealer reported that he had sold 300 cars during the year to fleet people alone, while a haberdasher reported that he had sold 80 suits of clothing to sailors in just one day.[8] Deliveries of fresh food and provisions to the naval ships in port were staggering. For example, 50,000 pounds of beef at $5,500; 35,000 dozen eggs at $6,300; and 385,000 pounds of potatoes at $7,700 were monthly costs for the fleet. Five hundred thousand pounds of provisions passed through Long Beach Landing alone every 24 hours.[9]

Business might have been even better for local merchants if much of what was supplied to the fleet had not been purchased in San Francisco and then shipped down the coast to L.A. harbor where the fleet was based the greater part of the year. A number of reasons account for this uneconomical manner of purchasing supplies. First of all, the Navy's Bureau of Supplies and Accounts had a branch office in the Bay area, and many naval officers favored San Francisco Bay as the best location for a permanent naval base; there was also a lack of storage space in Los Angeles harbor. But the most important reason that San Francisco concerns may have profitted from furnishing supplies to the San Pedro-Long Beach-based forces afloat was the political influence of California's two United States Senators, Hiram Johnson and Samuel Shortridge, both Bay Area Republicans. At least this latter reason was the view of the Los Angeles publication *Saturday Night,* which told its readers to vote for Democrat William Gibbs MacAdoo over Samuel Shortridge for senator in the upcoming election of 1932, and at the same time chided local Republicans and the Los Angeles Chamber of Commerce for being indifferent to the plight of Los Angeles suppliers.[10] Whatever the case, a San Pedro publication asked commercial interests to "do something vital about obtaining a branch of the Navy's Bureau of Supplies and Accounts" for the San Pedro area.[11]

A Christmas party for orphans on the USS Maryland. The youngsters received presents and a turkey dinner. HMB

Income property owners and other real estate interests were happy to hear that navy dependents and their personal goods were beginning to arrive in the area in great numbers when the home port of Scouting Force was officially changed from New York to San Pedro. Most families were headed for Long Beach, however.[12] Besides being bigger, Long Beach was preferred over San Pedro for "obvious reasons." Some factors involved may have been the presence of San Pedro's notorious Beacon Street with its flock of beer joints and fleet followers, loan sharks and gyp artists. Or maybe the smell of Fish Harbor was too much for the tender nostrils of navy families, for a common expression at the time was "Long Beach by the sea, San Pedro by the smell."[13] Nevertheless, some very fancy apartment houses did spring up in Point Fermin. This area was easily accessible to the officers' landing at Cabrillo Beach and had attractive harbor views. Some rental units were so exclusive as "to not allow any tenant under the rank of Commander." Housing remained hard to find anywhere, and in 1936 it was estimated that San Pedro was short one thousand dwellings.[14]

The shortages of housing brought the inevitable higher rents. In 1934 Admiral Harris Lanning authorized an official survey of the housing situation in the San Pedro Bay area and concluded that unless the situation was rectified, certain units of the fleet might have to be moved. A typical Seaman First Class making $62 usually paid $18 monthly rent for a bungalow court or apartment on Daisy or Cherry Avenues in Long Beach. When rent increased, he was forced to move to Wilmington or Compton.[15] Many servicemen accused landlords of raising rents because navy people could afford to pay and were less permanent than other tenants. The situation got so out of hand that the Long Beach Chamber of Commerce referred the matter to the Long Beach Apartment Owners Association and requested that unless they took action to stop this kind of discrimination, they would ruin the Chamber's efforts to entice large numbers of "navy personnel to live in Long Beach."[16]

In 1939, with the growing number of ships assigned to the area, pressure mounted for navy or public housing to alleviate the critical housing shortages. That same year, 300 low-cost housing units were offered, but only 100 of them were set aside for servicemen. The next year, homes in Carmelitos and Harbor Hills (Lomita) were made available to bluejackets who earned less than $100 a month or lived in sub-standard housing. Many of the lower pay grades would easily qualify because affordable apartments in Long Beach and San Pedro were substandard.[17]

In marked contrast to the plight of the enlisted men were the officers whose pay and social prestige allowed them to live in the best neighborhoods of both communities. Compared to civilian contemporaries, naval officers were paid well, and in many of the principal "home ports" around the country, an average Lieutenant could live in a rented two or three bedroom house and employ a full-time maid. When Ernest J. King, for example, assumed command of the aircraft carrier *Lexington* in 1930, he was able to find excellent quarters for himself and his family in the exclusive Bixby Park area of Long Beach.[18] Admiral James O. Richardson lived at the elegant Villa Riviera.

The fleet's presence was important in other areas as well. It played a vital role in relief operations during the devastating earthquake that struck Long Beach on 10 March, 1933. The potent tremor killed 54 people and severely injured hundreds more when it hit a little before six o'clock in the evening. Many buildings collapsed, and property damage was widespread. When the city's gas and power were shut off, Long Beach and environs fell into near panic.

The fleet was in port that night, and the nature of the disaster was sensed almost immediately by naval authorities when their ships began rolling violently. Three thou-

President-elect Herbert Hoover waiting to be taken to the USS Maryland from a San Pedro Landing. The Maryland would carry him on a good-will visit to Latin America in 1928. SP/LAPL

sand sailors and marines were quickly ordered into the city to render assistance. A large crevice in front of the Navy Landing complicated the problem of getting ashore. Large gangways were hurriedly put in place and relief operations were ready to commence in a relatively short time. The shore force included a complete hospital unit from the cruiser *Omaha,* electric relief crews, firefighting units, rescue parties, and able-bodied sailors and marines ready to keep law and order in the devastated city. Navy radio teams

The proximity of the battleship Anchorage *to the movie capital in Hollywood brought movie stars and film companies out to visit the fleet. In this picture taken in 1928, Will Rogers stands beside Admiral Taylor on board the* Pennsylvania. *CB*

U.S.S. Saratoga *at anchor in the San Pedro- Long Beach Roadstead, 1928. CB*

also assisted the commercial broadcasters in disseminating useful information.[19]

U.S. Fleet Commander Richard Leigh had ordered his men to prepare for just such a calamity two years before when he held talks with the mayors of some of the local communities. Careful planning had paid off, and the City was back to normal much earlier than expected. The navy's efficient handling of the earthquake emergency was a boon to relations with the City. The president of the Pacific Electric Transportation Company echoed the prevailing attitude among grateful citizens when he said, "We have the greatest navy in the world."

Up until that time, the citizens of Long Beach and the navy had not always been on the best of terms. There were continuing reports about housing discrimination and unfair treatment of sailors that date back to the early twenties. The navy's heroic action in the earthquake and the added number of ships being based off the City's beaches seem to have had a positive affect on civil-military relations The best example of this new respect for the navy was the City's reception for the crews of the Battle Force when they returned after a long cruise in November 1934. Los Angeles and Long Beach coordinated their efforts in a truly effusive manner. On 26 November, San Pedro hosted the navy by opening up its streets to a California-style parade and street dancing all with a Fiesta theme. The spotlight was transferred to Long Beach that night when the City's Chamber of Commerce and Naval Affairs Committee kicked off Fleet Week, a full week of entertainment honoring the navy. The festivities began aboard the flagship *New Mexico* with a nineteen gun salute for the Governor of the State of California. Dubbed "Neptune's Holiday," city officials provided a carnival, a vaudeville show, street dancing, and a beauty pageant in which Neptune's Queen would be selected.[20] On Saturday the Commander-in-Chief of the United States Fleet, Admiral Joseph M. Reeves, was honored at a banquet at the Pacific Coast Club, and a formal ball in his honor was given at the Municipal Auditorium. In return, the navy scheduled inter-fleet football games and illuminated its ships at night.

Naval rescue teams in Long Beach during the earthquake of 1933. HMB

The Long Beach Navy Landing. Completed in 1930, its name was changed in 1933 to Leigh's Landing in honor Admiral Richard Leigh. He commanded the navy relief operations during the devastating earthquake of 1933. LBHD

Sailors arriving at the navy landing in Long Beach offering help during the 1933 earthquake. LBHD

Sailors assisting civilian authorities during the Long Beach Earthquake of March, 1933. LBPL

CHAPTER FIVE

Naval Expansion and the Fight to Keep the Fleet in San Pedro

The ominous nature of international relations in the thirties forecasted the expansion of the American Navy. German and Japanese imperialism posed direct threats to the world's sea lanes that could not be ignored. Naval leaders began making plans for the expansion of the fleet and its support facilities. In 1934, the fleet was to be brought up to treaty strength under the Vincent Trammel Act. Monies from certain New Deal programs set up to lessen unemployment and stimulate the economy were also made available for national defense projects. For example, early in the New Deal, $238 million were allocated to the navy from appropriations set aside to provide jobs.[1] Funds were appropriated from low interest loans made available by the NRA (National Recovery Administration), from the PWA (Public Works Administration), and the WPA (Works Progress Administration). Money was also obtainable from SERA (State Emergency Relief Administration).

In early 1933, the Los Angeles Board of Harbor Commissioners approved a plan for the expansion and improvement of naval facilities on city-owned property in San Pedro. The most important project was the construction of a long overdue Fleet Landing at berths 56 and 57, located at the foot of the East Channel at 22nd Street.[2] Another important installation built for the navy at San Pedro was the target repair base located at City berths 37, 38, 39, and 40 in the West Channel. This so-called "long dock" included a mess room, galley, work and shower rooms, sleeping quarters, and a storage area for target screens. A welcome relief after the damaging winds of 1933, this small facility was used primarily to overhaul target screens, moor Base Force auxiliaries, and secure the battle fleet's ship's boat during target practice. By the time the fleet returned to port in November 1934, the "long dock" crew had constructed a jib easily able to handle the long timbers used for the floating targets. Garbage scowls, oil barges, a small tug, and other auxiliaries attached to the base improved conditions for the forces afloat with efficient garbage collection and mail deliveries. The more than 80 ships' boats once left in exposed clusters near the breakwater during target practice would now be moored at the safer "long dock." It has been said that the navy had never seen "cleaner boats and more gleaming woodwork than in the San Pedro-Long Beach area."[3] One observer sentimentally described the base as the spot:

> *Where the tugs and the honey boats moor and the Fleet repairs its shell torn targets, where the water is sometimes oily and the sea gulls are fat and the ebb tides leave the rocks slimy along Fort Mac.*[4]

The navy supply wharf at the foot of 22nd Street was enlarged, and the fleet transit shed at berth 57 was improved.

In another SERA project the Harbor Department improved conditions for the sailors based at San Pedro by extending 22nd Street. The Department supplied $18,876 in material while SERA contributed $45,700 in labor costs for a needed second approach to various naval activities in the Outer Harbor. The new highway extended westerly from 22nd Street Navy Landing. The westerly terminus of the new road was Mesa and Crescent Avenues. Other improvements made by local government agencies were the opening of the Fleet Post Office at Berth 57. The Board of Harbor Commissioners also made arrangements with the Pacific Electric Transit Company to run its cars from downtown San Pedro to the Navy Landing. They also reallocated Outer Harbor anchorage space by assigning 80% of the available berths to the fleet.[5]

The restoration of Navy or Trona Field

near Cabrillo Beach by the San Pedro Chamber of Commerce and the Los Angeles Playground and Recreation Commission helped to keep this convenient site available for fleet baseball and football competition. Two new gridirons were built. The Admiral Leigh Basketball Stadium across the street from the San Pedro Army-Navy YMCA and the Anderson Memorial Pool were also built to enable the sports-minded sailors to relax and play in San Pedro.

The San Pedro-Long Beach anchorage still lacked the traditional prerequisites for remaining the home of the navy's largest warships. There was no adequate supply center or nearby graving dock. Local merchants, Chambers of Commerce, and congressional leaders were continually concerned about the prospect that the fleet might be transferred elsewhere. They naturally worried that the loss of the fleet would be a severe blow to the local economy. They also

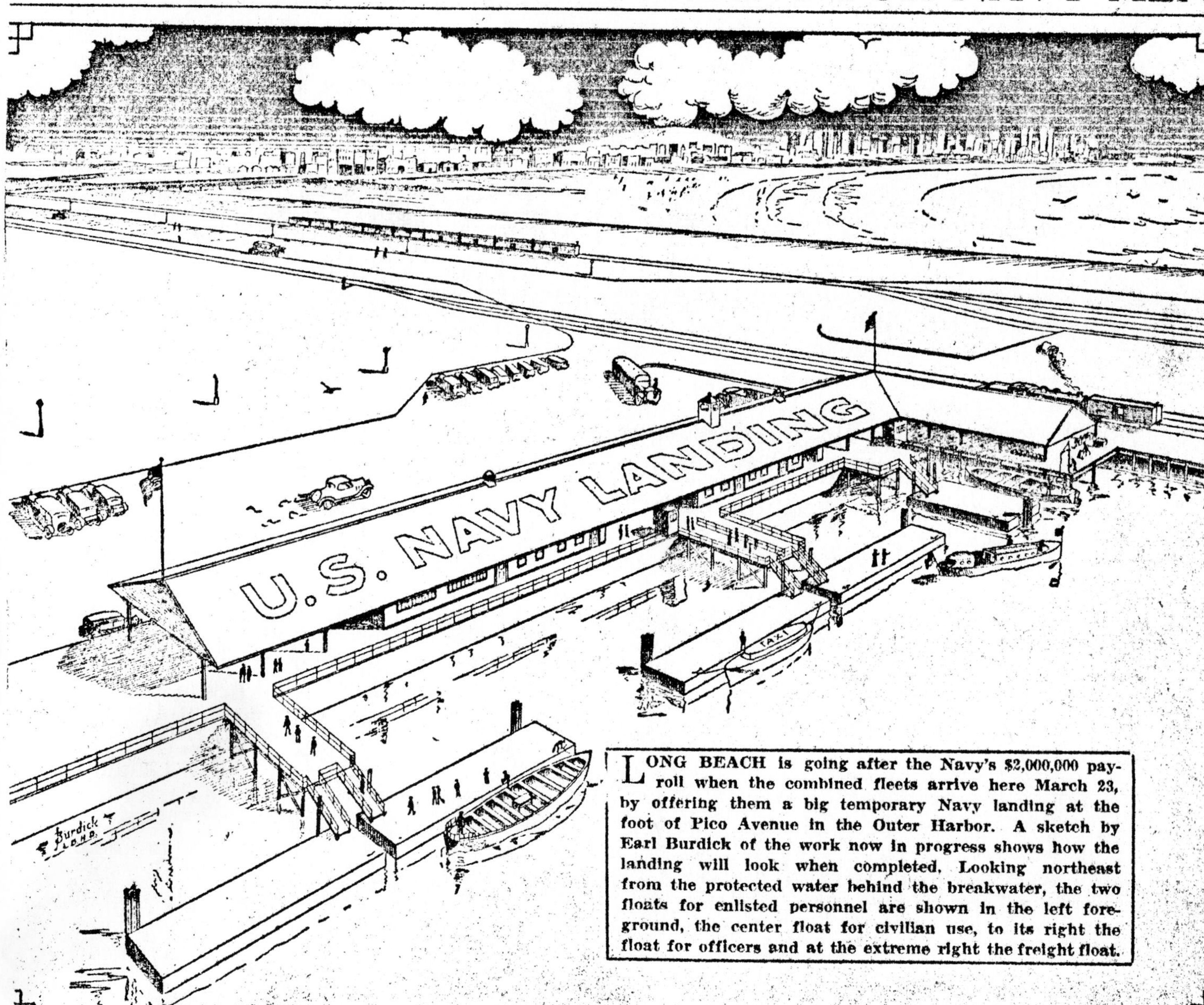

LONG BEACH PREPARES LANDING FOR NAVY MEN

LONG BEACH is going after the Navy's $2,000,000 payroll when the combined fleets arrive here March 23, by offering them a big temporary Navy landing at the foot of Pico Avenue in the Outer Harbor. A sketch by Earl Burdick of the work now in progress shows how the landing will look when completed. Looking northeast from the protected water behind the breakwater, the two floats for enlisted personnel are shown in the left foreground, the center float for civilian use, to its right the float for officers and at the extreme right the freight float.

Sketch of the Navy Landing at the foot of Pico Avenue in Long Beach. The name was changed to Leigh's Landing in honor of the Commander in Chief of the United States Fleet Richard Leigh after the earthquake of 1933. *HB*

Ships' boats being stored at the "Long Dock" in San Pedro's West Channel in 1934. *LAHD*

A ship's boat from the Medusa at the 22nd Street Navy Landing in October 1933. *LAHD*

believed that the construction and maintenance of adequate facilities would pump additional vigor into the economy. Local promoters were quick to point out that although the main units of the Battle Fleet were based at San Pedro Bay, only $700,000 had been spent there since California had come into the Union. In contrast, they pointed out that $182,000,000 had been funded for support activities in the San Francisco Bay area and $90,000,000 in San Diego during the same 85-year interval. One local booster bemoaned the port's fate when he wrote "although San Pedro is the base of the United States Fleet, there is hardly anything to indicate it."[6]

It would be an uphill battle to secure permanent shore facilities at San Pedro Bay. First of all, the three competing sites for a fleet base in the San Francisco Bay area pledged that they would unite in opposition to the selection of any fleet base in another region of the state. Furthermore, the drive to secure a Bay area base came from the formidable Senator Hiram Johnson and six-term representative Charles F. Curry. Finally, the navy itself continued to recommend, as it had steadfastly done since 1917, that a fleet base be established at Alameda in San Francisco Bay.[7]

Representative Charles J. Colden of San Pedro and others nevertheless fought hard to improve San Pedro's chances of remaining the home port of the Battle Fleet by trying to secure an important $14 million PWA harbor improvement grant. One of its major projects was a $5 million municipally-owned graving dock able to accommodate two battleships at the same time. The two docks would each be 1,000 feet long with 145-foot gate openings. Borings on a possible Outer Harbor site had already been taken, and there was general agreement that the proposed location was excellent. Tests showed it had hard rock overlaid by hard clay and a strata of shale. Admiral Richard Leigh, the Commander of the United States Fleet at that time, chose the San Pedro site

Ship's boats moored along the "Long Dock" in San Pedro's West Channel during target practice in January 1934. LAHD

over one in Long Beach for those reasons.[8] In Congress, Representative Colden simultaneously introduced a bill for the purchase of Navy Field from the Southern Pacific Railroad, proposing to call it the Mississippi Memorial Athletic Field.[9] The nucleus of a naval base projecting east from Cabrillo Beach seemed to be a distinct possibility in the near future.

The plan to insure the fleet's presence in San Pedro received a major setback, however, when the $14 million harbor improvement package was voted down on 25 November 1935. With only a 13% voter turnout, the measure missed passage by a mere 1881 votes.[10] While the port area supported the measure, the rest of the city opposed it. A WPA announcement cancelling the $5 million graving dock just before the election may have also influenced the negative vote. Harold Ickes, the chief administrator of the PWA, indicated that he had cancelled the project because his agency required that all projects be finished within a year's time. The dry dock's estimated time of construction was 18 months. In a terse article in the San Pedro *News Pilot* entitled "Explanation Seems Due," Ickes was accused of ineptitude. The writer suggested that not only did the PWA's chief administrator know about the needed 18 months of construction time, he also knew that the dock could be built in a year if needed. The real reason why Ickes scuttled the San Pedro drydock, according to the article, was to placate Senator Hiram Johnson and other Bay area congressmen who saw the San Pedro dock as a threat to the development of a fleet base in the Bay area.[11]

Representative Colden and others continued to press the Naval Affairs Committee of the House of Representatives for the expansion of shore facilities on San Pedro Bay. They were rebuffed again by Chief of the Bureau of Navigation, Rear Admiral William D. Leahy. Leahy told the Committee that "the Navy Department does (did) not need a navy yard at San Pedro at the present time" and that it could use the money for other projects. Leahy also pointed out that the West Coast was already being serviced by two good yards at Mare Island and Puget Sound, and both of them could provide the needed overhauls for most of the large ships on the Pacific Coast. Certain vessels of the Scouting Force, however, would have to return to East Coast yards for refitting. Without mentioning the political consequences of closing those yards, he told the Committee that any dislocation of the skilled force of artisans there would not be good for national security. He also told the Committee that the navy had already begun overhauls at Pearl Harbor where a strong nucleus of artisans was forming.[12]

With growing Japanese aggression in China in 1937, President Roosevelt began pushing for stepped up naval expansion. Included in the Vincent-Trammel Act of 1938 were added funds for naval yards and other installations. While some groups in San Pedro favorably received Roosevelt's commitment to create a navy second to none, others feared that commercial growth would be squeezed out by the navy in an "already overtaxed harbor." The future of the navy airfield at Terminal Island, midway between San Pedro and Long Beach, became the focal point of a struggle between some local interests and the navy.

Developed in 1928 by the City of Los Angeles as a public field, Allen Airport was taken over by the navy in 1935 under a thirty-year lease with the Harbor Department. It was a facility for servicing the shipboard aircraft of the battleships and cruisers based in San Pedro Bay. There was also some talk about using the field to service carrier aircraft from the Long Beach assigned carriers *Lexington* and *Saratoga*.[13] In 1935 the air facility was renamed Reeves Field after the air-minded Commander-in-Chief of the United States Fleet, Joseph Mason Reeves. Further development of the field was begun under a WPA relief appropriation program, and in May 1937 the readied air base was turned over to the Commander, Aircraft Battle Force. By then the joint WPA-Harbor Department project included a 255-acre field, a 640-foot overhaul apron, a 286-foot concrete seaplane ramp, a 225-foot dock, a 1400-foot breakwater, a 9200-foot long, 400-foot wide landscape runway, highways, water and electric facilities, and a dredged seaplane anchorage.[14] On 1 March 1938, Reeves Field was upgraded to the status of a Fleet Air Base. By mid-June 1938, the base was servicing 130 observation aircraft and had a complement of 60 officers and 300 men. More expansion of the air field was anticipated, and by June 1939 it based 200 aircraft and had a complement of 100 officers and 600 enlisted men.[15] The navy began actively seeking outright ownership of

The 22nd Street Navy Landing in June 1935: Construction funds came from programs set up under agencies of the New Deal. LAHD

Admiral Joseph M. Reeves and officials of the LA Harbor Commission at the commissioning of Reeves Field on Terminal Island, in 1936. Up-graded to the status of a Fleet Air Base in 1938, the property was returned to the City of Los Angeles in the mid-sixties. LAHD

the field to free congressional appropriations held up by a rule that limited the construction of "permanent" facilities on installations now owned by the navy.

The Los Angeles and San Pedro Chambers of Commerce and the San Pedro Junior Chamber of Commerce supported the unconditional cession of Reeves Field to the Federal Government. Many were convinced that outright navy ownership of the field might be the final "weighty factor in clinching the U.S. Fleet for this port."[16] The Harbor Commission of the City of Los Angeles, on the other hand, saw the matter quite differently. At first the Commission's Chairman, Arthur Eldridge, opposed ceding the field to the government because some of the acreage to be used by the navy was vital for port development. In an apparent compromise, however, Eldridge later recommended that the City's voters should decide on whether or not to grant the land. Opponents of an outright grant did not want to lose oil revenues or curtail port development.[17] They also insisted that the navy should return the property when it was no longer needed. Thus began a Navy-City debate which lasted well over a year.

On 2 May 1939 the voters of the City of Los Angeles authorized the proposed transfer of the title of the Terminal Island property. The City, however, imposed several restrictions on the deed transfer to the navy. The Harbor Commission wanted the Federal Government to pay the "fair price" of $10 million in compensation for the future loss of port commercial development. They also wanted to retain oil rights and have the ability to develop nearby offshore harbor construction. They insisted most emphatically that the City should resume title if the navy did not use the base for a period of more than 12 consecutive months. The City also asked that a 50 foot strip along the field's northern boundary be reserved for oil drilling and that there be southwesterly post development even if it conflicted with navy plans. The 50-foot strip was on the approach to the landing field, and the port development clashed with navy plans to further develop its seaplane anchorage.[18]

In negotiations with the navy, the City would not back down on any of the deed restrictions. The Los Angeles Harbor Commission resolved that it needed both the oil revenues for future port growth and new berths southwest of the field for the larger ships of the future. The Commission played down the navy's objections to oil drilling along the field's northern approach. They indicated that only one drilling derrick would be there at a time, and that when the well was in production it would be replaced by a "Christmas Tree" configuration that would not exceed the height of any of the surrounding navy structures. The Mayor of Los Angeles, Fletcher Bowron, confidentially told a radio audience that because of the airfield's ideal location, there was "no fear the navy will (would) turn elsewhere." He also explained to his constituents that the recent vote by the people of Los Angeles did not authorize the transfer of Reeves Field without strings attached, but vested the mayor and the City Council with the leverage to protect the community's vital interests. While reaffirming his belief in the need for a big navy, he felt that the interests of the people of Los Angeles came first. "My patriotic fervor," he exclaimed, "cannot override sober judgement."[19]

The controversy dragged on after World War II had broken out on 1 September 1939. A ranking member of the House Naval Affairs Committee, Melvin J. Maas of Minnesota, responding to the pressing need to build up American naval forces quickly, called for an immediate agreement over the airfield property without qualifications. And "If we seek a new field," he threatened, "we will have to find a new anchorage as well."[20] But the City still held firm. When the navy asked local authorities to stop its plans for oil drilling off the southwest corner of the main runway because it endangered flight operations, Harbor Commissioner Glen Arbogast replied that to do so was "an impossible requirement."[21]

The navy's attempt to increase its shore activities in San Pedro's Outer Harbor was also difficult to negotiate. The navy wanted the entire Outer Harbor south of 22nd Street, especially the six-story municipal storehouse known as Pier One. The City spurned the navy's request for the purchase or lease of the 450,000-square foot property because it was the only facility that it had that was fireproof. The City also did not have any other dock that could take deep draft ships. One Harbor Commissioner stated that it would be unwise to give the navy Pier One unless the Federal Government gave assurances that it would deepen another slip. However, the Commissioners reluctantly

The YC 16, one of the fleet's "honey boats" making its appointed rounds of ships anchored in the roadstead. ON

District Patrol vessel 39 underway in San Pedro's West Channel. This craft frequently served fleet camera parties. ON

Sailors constructing target frames at the Target Base in the West Channel in 1937. ON

agreed to help the navy in an emergency or at least help them locate somewhere else in the port. Sensing the deteriorating relations between the navy and the City, and aware that the navy did have other options, Congressman Lee E. Geyer, a strong proponent of naval expansion, wired Mayor Bowron that "Unless the navy can (could) purchase Pier One at a low figure," it will lose the fleet and all the harbor improvements to Long Beach.[22]

Important decisions were being made in Washington, especially after the Fall of France in May 1940. In June, Congress appropriated $97,650,362 and $202,654,000 for the expansion of shore facilities alone. Included were funds for $19,750,000 for a naval complex in the San Pedro-Long Beach area.[23] Persistent rumors circulated that the Federal Government might divest the City of Los Angeles of its Reeves Field property through a condemnation procedure and then build a 1092-foot dry dock and other facilities on the Long Beach side of Terminal Island. Undaunted by these rumors, San Pedro forces worked tirelessly to secure the lion's share of the new navy appropriations for their portion of the harbor. Harry Carr, spokesman of the San Pedro Citizen's Executive Committee, which was backed by local businessmen, proposed that the Harbor Commission sell Reeves Field and Pier One to the navy immediately. They also called for giving the navy the West Channel graving dock site free of charge. These offers were of no use. On 9 August 1940 the Federal Government officially condemned both the Los Angeles-owned 228 acres making up Reeves Field and an adjacent 105 acres in Long Beach. This Long Beach property was also south of Seaside Avenue and extended from the western border of Reeves Field as far east as the Long Beach Channel. Los Angeles would be allowed to sue for compensation at a later time. Boasting that it was "glad to cooperate with Washington regardless of compensation," Long Beach ceded to the Federal Government its mostly undeveloped land-fill portion of Terminal Island for $1. The City was nonetheless sued in the

The officers and men of the Target Base in San Pedro's West Channel in 1937. ON

The Long Beach Naval Shipyard and the Long Beach Naval Station as it developed in the war and post-war years. LBPL

action to insure immediate government possession.[24]

The controversial selection of the eastern end of Terminal Island for the location of the large graving dock might well have been motivated by the strident relations between the navy and the City of Los Angeles. But Long Beach had been favored over San Pedro by most of the naval commanders who had been stationed in the area over the years. In the early twenties, Admiral Eberle chose to make his headquarters there. As the second breakwater neared completion in 1936, the Flagship of the U.S. Fleet *Pennsylvania* changed its anchorage closer to Long Beach instead of its customary berth inside the San Pedro breakwater. When the Battle Force Flagship *California* and the Battleship Division's Flagship *West Virginia* returned to port, they also moved to new positions off Long Beach.[25] With the completion of the second breakwater, only repair ships and auxiliaries remained off San Pedro. Long Beach had truly become the home of the battleships and the site of "battleship row." But Long Beach had an even greater asset in becoming the site for San Pedro Bay's new naval complex. It was adjacent to the Naval Air Station, and air power was already making its mark in the current struggle in Europe. An enlarged airfield with nearby administrative and recreational facilities was only possible in Long Beach. Cross-channel commuting between bases in Terminal Island and San Pedro was neither practical or convenient.

The large graving dock to be built on Terminal Island was first known as the Bethlehem Dry Dock because the navy had originally contracted with that company for construction of the dock in 1940. When the entire project became broader in scope, it was variously called the Terminal Island Naval Dry Docks and the Moreel Dock, after the Navy's Director of Yards and Docks. The entire complex, including a complete naval shipyard and operating base, was designated Roosevelt Base, Terminal Island, California, on 7 May 1941.[26]

Expanding Berth 57 in May 1939. The San Pedro Army and Navy YMCA is to the left of the smoke stack. LAHD

CHAPTER SIX

The Fleet Prepares for War

During the inter-war period, Japan was considered America's most likely foe in a Pacific war. This view was reinforced by both Japan's militaristic past and her belligerent behavior in the 1930's. Plan Orange, America's naval response to a Japanese onslaught in the western Pacific, was devised and studied by the Navy's General Board and the Naval War College. If war seemed imminent, the United States Fleet would concentrate in Hawaiian waters and then engage Japanese forces in a classic naval battle. The big ships of the Battle Fleet were the core of American strategic thinking. Though the plan was revised to also include economic strangulation of the Japanese home islands, the battleships and cruisers of the U.S. Fleet remained at the center of any encounter with the Island Empire. It was for this reason that top naval. billets went to officers who had gunnery and battleship experience. Representative Carl Vinson of the Naval Affairs Committee restated this belief when he said the American navy's battleships gave "evidence of tangible national strength."

Admiral Joseph Mason Reeves, the Commander-in-Chief of the United States Fleet in the mid-thirties, agreed with many naval officers of his generation that a war with Japan would probably start with a "Port-Arthur-like" sneak attack on the American fleet wherever it was assembled. Reeves succeeded in making his command more security-conscious when he ordered armed watches and posted armed sentries at naval docks.[1] Reeves first demonstrated this security-mindedness in 1934 when he ordered the fleet to move quickly through the Canal Zone after it was reported that there was a plot to blow up the canal. In a bold training maneuver in 1935, Reeves ordered without warning the fleet's "expeditious departure" from its San Pedro anchorage on a Saturday afternoon. With only 25% of the crews aboard, the fleet steamed out of port in battle formation and rendezvoused with San Diego-based units 150 miles west of Point Loma, California. Many of the battleships, some under command of junior officers, had indeed sought safety from a presumed Japanese "sneak" attack.[2] Reeves ordered another "expeditious departure" on a Friday afternoon in 1936 just as crewmen were readying themselves for week-end liberty. Included in the drill was a communications blackout, with the Base Force Flagship *Argonne* ordered not to receive any telephone calls. Official messages were to be handled only through the naval radio station on Trona Field. At 3:45, the carriers were the first ships to clear port. The battleships left next, followed by the Fleet Train.[3] A total of 30 San Pedro-based ships met San Diego units this time off San Clemente. With the exception of a few stragglers, the twin ports were emptied of naval craft by sundown. Thousands of ships' personnel were left stranded on the beach overnight, and according to one report, some ships' boats engaged in various tasks were left high and dry. In this exercise, San Diego-based aricraft made their first sunset landings on the Long Beach-based carriers *Lexington* and *Saratoga*.[4] The drill was hailed as a "tactical success of high propaganda value," because the navy used "every secrecy measure of actual war." The exercise was over within 24 hours when the repair ship *Vestal,* last to leave port, became the first to return. The disruption of the ladies' so-called "table fleet ashore," was easily resumed that evening.[5]

One of the most incredible exercises that the fleet participated in began on 4 January 1939, when the heavy ships left port for a Fleet Problem in the Caribbean-Atlantic zone. With tensions in Europe at the breaking point, the activities of the U.S. Fleet began to receive greater national attention and news coverage. The *Long Beach*

Press Telegram mirrored this trend by honoring the departing warriors with several pages dedicated to the officers and enlisted men of the fleet. It was more than local interest in the navy; this attention underscored the growing awareness everywhere that in time of peril, the fleet was America's first line of defense. The coverage in the *Press Telegram* was very thorough, giving a complete list of the ships and officers of the U.S. Fleet in a section entitled "Officers of Battleship Row." Included were Rear Admiral Chester W. Nimitz, commanding a battleship division from the *Arizona;* Vice-Admiral Ernest J. King, flying his flag on the *Saratoga;* Captain Raymond A. Spruance, commanding the battleship *Mississippi*, and Rear Admiral Husband E. Kimmel, aboard a cruiser flagship *San Francisco.*[6] These men were all destined to make history after America's entrance into the Second World War. Known as Fleet Problem XX, the exercise took the mighty fleet to the Atlantic for manuevers. The training mission was to be concluded with a majestic naval review off New York City, planned to coincide with the opening of the New York World's Fair on 29 April 1939.

Admiral James O. Richardson taking command of the Battle Force in San Pedro-Long Beach on 24 June 1939. *NHD*

Rear Admiral Chester W. Nimitz taking command of Battleship Division 1 (BATDIV-1) aboard the USS Arizona in the late 1930's. *HMB*

Bugler positioned before 16 inch guns of a Maryland class battleship. ON

Events in Europe, however, took a turn for the worse when Italy invaded Albania and Hitler readied himself for an assault on the remainder of Czechoslovakia. Fearing that the fleet's Atlantic concentration would encourage Japanese advances in the Pacific, President Roosevelt unexpectedly cancelled the naval review and ordered the fleet back to its West Coast bases. It was hoped that the fleet's return to the Pacific would ease Australia's fears and strengthen the hands of those elements in Japan who were wary of a possible military pact with Germany.[7] Admiral William F. Halsey, on the other hand, believed that the call back to the Pacific was a response to reports that the Japanese were plotting to blow up the Panama Canal around 1 July.

The Battle Force arrived back at the San Pedro-Long Beach roadstead on 12 May 1939 with much fanfare. At 7 a.m., the fleet flagship *Pennsylvania* nosed its way through a thin veil of haze southwest of Catalina Island and moved gracefully to its anchorage. Spanning the *Nevada* and the *Arizona* were the *West Virginia, New Mexico, Idaho,* and the *Mississippi,* all forming a line close to the breakwater. The *Oklahoma* resumed its position behind the *Idaho.* The heavy cruisers *Houston, Northampton, Minneapolis, New Orleans, Portland,* and *Indianapolis* moved closer to the shore, the latter gliding close to the Navy Landing within the Long Beach breakwater. Entering the port for the first time were the new cruisers *Boise* and *Phoenix,* both replacing Cruiser Division Seven, which was ordered to remain in the troubled Atlantic. Over 300,000 people watched the ships anchor at prearranged anchorages and kedges, while newsreel coverage guaranteed world-wide notice of American naval power.[8]

The Naval Affairs Committee of the Long Beach Chamber of Commerce planned a week-long celebration commemorating the fleet's safe return. Theaters, skating palaces, and other places of entertainment were thrown open to sailors free of charge. A

Fleet at anchor during mid-1930's. Long Beach and Southern California mountains in the distance. *LBHD*

special carnival with 14 vaudeville acts was staged at the Long Beach Municipal Auditorium. Banners and buntings were strung along the main boulevards leading to the Navy Landing. Jovial Long Beach was getting national and even world-wide attention with its generous welcome of the fleet.[9]

San Pedro was not as gracious to the men in blue. In years past, she had been. The only plans for the fleet homecoming was a dance at the Fleet Reserve Clubhouse. Tige Clinton, the *San Pedro News Pilot* maritime affairs columnist, bitterly observed that the harbor was a "No-man's land" to the City of Los Angeles except at tax time, and that the City's "official welcome" of the fleet "ought to be listed as Los Angeles' No. 1 shame."[10]

As instability in both Europe and Asia increased in tempo, the navy naturally began tightening fleet security further. Concern ranged all the way from anxieties about surprise attack by submarines, aircraft, and surface ships to harbor mining, sabotage and spying. The activities of visiting Japanese-registered tankers and freighters and locally based Japanese-American owned fishing boats were studied. Unfortunately, the two were never clearly differentiated in the minds of some naval officers. Captain William F. Halsey, for example, commanding the Long Beach based carrier *Saratoga,* was convinced that many Japanese tankers that frequented the ports were also spy ships because they were handled in "navy fashion." He also believed that Japanese-American fishing boats deliberately operated near naval training sites for purposes of spying.[11]

In late September 1940, anti-Japanese feeling approached near epidemic proportions when it was rumored in Washington that the Japanese fishing village near Reeves Field was the nerve center of a vast foreign espionage ring. Representative Leo Geyer, a leading proponent of expanding naval activities in San Pedro Bay, called for the removal of all aliens living on Terminal Island. Of the estimated 3000 Japanese living near the airfield, a great many were foreign born. While the navy indicated that it was not asking for their removal, one official did state that their evacuation would at last "clarify the situation."[12] The Federal Government did, however, impose restrictions upon alien-operated fishing and pleasure craft within the harbor. There was also a flurry of suspicion when a group of Japanese-Americans made inquiries about the purchase of Trona Navy Athletic Field when it was put up for sale by the Southern Pacific Railroad.[13] After Japan attacked Pearl Harbor on 7 December 1941, the Japanese-Americans living on Terminal Island had the dubious distinction of being the first victims of relocation. The government justified their removal on the grounds

Japanese fisherman's village on Terminal Island. Their proximity to naval facilities and ships was the subject of controversy before America's entrance into the Second World War. SP/LAPL

that the area they lived in had to be condemned for military and strategic purposes. The panic-stricken community's departure from Terminal Island was unfortunately a forewarning of the further evacuation of all Japanese-Americans from the West Coast after the U.S. entered the Second World War.[14]

When Admiral James O. Richardson assumed command of the United States Fleet in early 1940, security measures were made even more stringent. A general letter was circulated covering regulations on shipboard visitors, the safeguarding of both confidential and secret papers aboard ship, observation of shore boats and small craft, scrutiny of packages brought on board ship, disclosures of classified information, photographing of ships, reporting the movements of foreign ships, and providing special protection for powder magazine. Armed personnel watches were also emphasized.[15] Nobody could deny that the security of the fleet had to be tightened during the more than two-year period that the United States remained on the sidelines during the Second World War. But the mild hysteria that came with the numerous false alarms about the imminence of war or attack had some adverse effects. Crews became tense and overworked, and after a while many "cries of wolf" made them impervious to these warnings.[16]

On 1 April 1940, the battleships and cruisers of the United States Fleet left their anchorages in two main bodies and sailed for training exercises off the Hawaiian Islands. These maneuvers were slated to last from 8 April to 9 May. At the time of departure, few would have imagined that this sortie would bring an end to the era of basing the capital ships of the United States Fleet along San Pedro Bay's "battleship row." Still fewer could imagine the fate awaiting these men-of-war at their new station, Pearl Harbor, Oahu. Roosevelt and his advisers, believing that American naval power at Pearl Harbor might deter Japanese encroachments in the Western Pacific, ordered the fleet to remain in Hawaiian waters after the war games were over. The fall of France had destabilized the Western Pacific where Japan seemed ready to move against French and Dutch possessions.[17]

Admiral James O. Richardson did not agree with Roosevelt's deterrent policy. He felt that the Hawaiian deployment was hurting the fleet's efficiency and that preparation for war could best be done at West Coast ports. His concern was not that the Japanese would attack the fleet at Pearl Harbor, but that the extended deployment was curtailing fleet training. He complained that gunnery schedules had fallen behind because all the tugs, target rafts, and target planes were back on the West Coast. He was also unhappy about crew morale and the inadequate berthing conditions at both Pearl Harbor and Lahaina Roads. Richardson flew to Washington, D.C. in early July 1940 to bring his case before the President. Although he could not convince President Roosevelt that bringing the fleet back to its West Coast ports would not be viewed by the Japanese as evidence of America's lack of resolve, he did win approval for a temporary return of the fleet to its home ports for leaves, docking, and taking on ammunition and stores. FDR also agreed to bring ships' complements up to wartime levels.[18]

The fleet was brought back to the West Coast in three staggered contingents of equal size, each to remain in port for about two weeks. The destroyers and carriers would return to San Diego, while the battleships and cruisers would anchor in Long Beach. The first contingent arrived in Long Beach on 30 September 1940. The temporary flagship of the U.S. Fleet, the *New Mexico,* and battleships *Oklahoma, Arizona, Mississippi,* and *Idaho* and a pair of cruisers easily found their way to familiar moorings. The *Saratoga* fired a 17 gun salute to Admiral Richardson, and the *New Mexico* returned its salute. Earlier, Richardson had requested that no special social functions be made commemorating the return of the warships. For many sailors, it was a quiet return to their family and homes. One observer noted the "stiff stern looks on the faces of the homecoming sailors."[19] One unmarried blue jacket exclaimed, "I sure cussed this place (Long Beach) but I had to get away to appreciate it." During the task force's short stay, over 2500 new recruits and replacements had boarded the ship by the time it sailed for Hawaii on 14 October.[20] The *New Mexico, Idaho,* and *Mississippi* would shortly be transferred to the Atlantic Fleet and would survive the war. The *Arizona* would return once again to the Coast for an overhaul and then become the severist casualty of the Pearl Harbor attack on 7 December 1941. The *Oklahoma* would also sink in the attack.

B-17 bombers flying over the naval anchorage shortly before the fleet left for Pearl Harbor. Note that battleship anchorages were farther out and closer to the breakwater than the cruisers. DWHA

The second group of ships returned on 20 October. This force included the battleships *West Virginia, Maryland* and *Colorado,* three cruisers, and some auxiliaries.[21] During the attack on Pearl Harbor, the *West Virginia* took many torpedoes and was sunk; the *Maryland,* moored inboard from the *Oklahoma,* suffered only slight damage; the *Colorado* was not at Pearl Harbor on that fateful morning. The last group arrived in mid-November in time for Thanksgiving. This force included the *California,* the *Tennessee,* the *Oklahoma* once again, and three cruisers.[22] The *Nevada* had come separately. This group left almost unnoticed after its brief holiday stay. At Pearl Harbor on 7 December, the *California* sank after a three day struggle to keep afloat, and the *Tennessee,* protected by the *West Virginia,* survived the fires from the burning debris of the *Arizona.* The *Nevada* made a dramatic sortie in the harbor during the attack but went aground.[23]

Of all the battleships that were homeported in San Pedro Bay in the inter-war period, as most of them were, seven were not at Pearl Harbor, three were sunk, one capsized, and four were damaged in the attack. The ships that were sunk or crippled during the attack met a fate on that dreadful Sunday that could never have been imagined in those peacetime years when the Battle Fleet lay at anchor in San Pedro-Long Beach and its primary concerns were weekend liberty, gunnery scores, fleet athletic competitions, and the various mundane happenings of a peacetime navy.

USS Lexington (CV-2) and USS Saratoga (CV-3) anchored beyond the second breakwater off Long Beach in the late 1930's. SP/LAPL

Fleet at anchor as viewed from Long Beach's Rainbow Pier. Catalina Island is in the distance. *LBPL*

The Pennsylvania, *flagship of the United States Fleet, in Long Beach, California, in 1936.* *USN*

USS California (BB-44). Between 1921 and 1941 this battleship served as the Flagship of the Pacific Fleet and the Flagship of the Battle Force of the United States Fleet. *USNI*

Mid-thirties panorama of United States Fleet at rest in San Pedro Bay. Note USS Saratoga anchored beyond the incompleted breakwater extension. HVB

FOOTNOTES

Chapter I

[1]Henry A. Wiley, *An Admiral From Texas* (New York: Doran and Company, 1934), p. 231.

[2]*Long Beach Press-Telegram,* August 9, 1919.

[3]*Autobiography of William V. Pratt, USN,* Washington D.C.: Navy History Division, Chapter XV, p. 10.

[4]*Board of Harbor Commissioners Report for the Port of Los Angeles,* 1925, p. 46.

[5]Pratt, *op. cit.,* Chapter XVII, pg. 5.

[6]"Preliminary Report of Navy Yard Commission," 64th Congress, 2nd Session, House of Representatives, Document no. 1946, 1916, p. 19.

[7]U.S. Senate Subcommittee on Appropriations, *Hearings,* 1922, p. 324.

[8]"San Pedro's Target Repair Base," *Our Navy,* Mid-September, 1937, p. 16.

[9]Wiley, *op. cit.,* p. 238.

[10]Gerald E. Wheeler, *Prelude to Pearl Harbor: The United States Navy and the Far East, 1921-1931* (Columbia: University of Missouri Press), p. 112.

Chapter II

[1]U.S. House of Representatives, *A Preliminary Examination of the Los Angeles and Long Beach Harbors,* 68th Congress, First Session, 1924, Document 349, p. 86.

[2]*Long Beach Press-Telegram,* March 17, 1928.

[3]*Ibid.,* October 30, 1928.

[4]*Autobiography of William V. Pratt, USN* (Washington D.C. Navy History Division), Chapter XVIII, p. 15.

[5]*Long Beach Press-Telegram,* January 11, 1933.

[6]Robert G. Wells, "Long Beach's Great Barrier Reef," *Southland Magazine, Long Beach Press-Telegram,* January 29, 1956, p. 3.

[7]*Ibid.*

[8]*Long Beach Press-Telegram,* September 29, 1939.

[9]Truman P. Riddle, "Enlisted Men's Families," *Proceedings of the United States Naval Institute,* January, 1939, p. 83.

[10]Gerald E. Wheeler, *Admiral William Veazie Pratt: A Sailor's Life* (Washington D.C. Naval History Division, 1974), p. 219.

[11]Yates Stirling, *Sea Duty: The Memoirs of a Fighting Admiral* (New York: G.P. Putnam's Sons, 1939), p. 192.

[12]Henry A. Wiley, *An Admiral From Texas* (New York: Doran and Company, 1934), p. 238.

[13]Wheeler, *op. cit.,* p. 162.

[14]Pratt, *op. cit.,* Chapter XX, p. 5.

[15]*Annual Report of the Commander-in-Chief, United States Fleet, 1931-1932,* Washington D.C. National Archives and Record Service, 1974, p. 34.

[16]Wiley, *op. cit.,* pp. 245-51.

[17]*Popular Science Magazine,* August 1934, p. 104.

[18]Wheeler, *op. cit.,* p. 234.

Chapter III

[1]Michael D. Reagan, "The Far Eastern Crisis of 1931-32: Stimson, Hoover and the Armed Services," in Harold Stein, *American Civil-Military Decisions* (University of Alabama Press, 1963), p. 34.

[2]Thaddeus V. Tuleja, *Statesman and Admirals: Quest for a Far Eastern Naval Policy* (New York: WW Norton & Company, Inc., 1963) pp. 72-73.

[3]Gerald E. Wheeler, *Admiral William Veazie Pratt: A Sailor's Life* (Washingtin D.C. Naval History Division, 1974), p. 348.

[4]Tuleja, *op. cit.,* p. 77.

[5]*Long Beach Press-Telegram,* April 18, 1932.

[6]William B. Standley and Arthur Agerton, *Admiral Ambassador to Russia* (Chicago: Henry Regenery Company, 1955), p. 27-28.

[7]Thomas B. Buell, *Master of Sea Power: A Biography of Fleet Admiral Ernest J. King* (Boston: Little Brown and Company, 1980), p. 90.

Chapter IV

[1]*Long Beach Press-Telegram,* October 29, 1934.

[2]James H. Collins, "The Fleet in Cold Cash," *Southern California Business,* November 1934, p. 19.

[3]Patrick Albazia, *Mr. Roosevelt's Navy: The Private War of the US Atlantic Fleet, 1939-1942,* (Annapolis: Naval Institute Press, 1975), p. 31.

[4]*Long Beach Press-Telegram,* December 31, 1932.

[5]*Ibid.,* November 2, 1932.

[6]*Southern California Business, op. cit.,* p. 18.

[7]*Ibid.,* p. 19.

[8]*Long Beach Press-Telegram,* December 31, 1932.

[9]*Ibid.*

[10]"How Los Angeles is Misserved," *Saturday Night Magazine,* August 6, 1932, p. 3.

[11]*San Pedro News Pilot,* May 19, 1936.

[12]*Long Beach Press-Telegram,* October 29, 1934.

[13]Interview with B.H. Brittingham, December 2, 1978.

[14]*San Pedro News Pilot,* October 2, 1972.

[15]*Our Navy,* August, 1939, p. 5.

[16]*Long Beach Press-Telegram,* November 8, 1934.

[17]*Our Navy,* September 15, 1940, pp. 10-11.

[18]Ernest J. King and Walter Muir Whitehall, *Fleet Admiral King. A Naval Record* (New York: Norton publishing Co., 1952), p. 217.

[19]*Long Beach Press-Telegram,* March 26, 1933.

[20]"Sailors Go To Town," *National Motorist,* January 1935. *Long Beach Press-Telegram,* November 9, 1934.

Chapter V

[1]William H. Standley and Arthur Agerton, *Admiral Ambassador to Russia* (Chicago: Henry Regenery Company, 1955), p. 31.

[2]*Annual Report of the Board of Harbor Commissioners,* Los Angeles, 1933, p. 83.

[3]"San Pedro's Target Repair Base," *Our Navy,* Mid-September, 1937, p. 18.

[4]*Our Navy,* February ?, 1940, p. 40.

[5]E.J. Amar, "The City Enlarges the Navy's Home," in *Southern California Business,* November 1934, p. 12.

[6]*San Pedro News Pilot,* January 13, 1936.

[7]See Frederic L. Paxon, "The Naval Station at Alameda 1916-1940," *Pacific Historical Review,* September 1944, pp. 235-250.

[8]*San Pedro News Pilot,* June 6, 1935.

[9]*Ibid.,* November 26, 1935.

[10]*Long Beach Press-Telegram,* November 27, 1935.

[11]*San Pedro News Pilot,* December 11, 1935.

[12]*Los Angeles Time,* July 31, 1937.

[13]*Our Navy,* June 1937, p. 54.

[14]*Los Angeles Times,* May 14, 1937.

[15]*Ibid.,* October 9, 1938.

[16]*San Pedro News Pilot,* April 25, 1939.

[17]*Ibid.,* January 18, 1938.

[18]*Los Angeles Times,* July 7, 1939.

[19]*Ibid.,* July 29, 1939.

[20]*Ibid.,* September 22, 1939.

[21]*Ibid.,* June 5, 1940.

[22]*San Pedro News Pilot,* June 22, 1940.

[23]U.S. Bureau of Yards and Docks, *Building the Navy's Bases in World War II* (Washington D.C. G.P.O., 1947), Vol. I, p. 171.

[24]*San Pedro News Pilot,* August 10, 1940.

[25]*Los Angeles Examiner,* August 26, 1936.

[26]Long Beach Naval Station, "What it is and how it got that way," n.d.

Chapter VI

[1]John D. Hayes, "Admiral Joseph Mason Reeves, USN, Part II — 1931-1948," *Naval War College Review,* January, 1972, p. 57.

[2]Daniel V. Gallery, *Eight Bells, and All's Well* (New York: W.W. Norton & Co., Inc., 1965), pp. 92-93.

[3]*San Pedro News Pilot,* March 21, 1936.

[4]John D. Hayes, *op. cit.,* p. 58.

[5]*San Pedro News Pilot,* March 21, 1936.

[6]*Long Beach Press Telegram, Annual 1939 Edition,* January 3, 1939.

[7]William L. Langer and S. Everett Gleason, *The Challenge of Isolation* (New York: Harper & Brothers Publishers, 1952), p. 104.

[8]*Long Beach Press Telegram,* May 12, 1939.

[9]*Ibid.,* May 11, 1939.

[10]*San Pedro News Pilot,* May 12, 1939.

[11]William F. Halsey and J. Bryan III, *Admiral Halsey's Story* (New York: McGraw-Hill Book Company, Inc., 1947), p. 64.

[12]*Long Beach Press Telegram,* September 28, 1940.

[13]*Our Navy,* December 1, 1940.

[14]Roger Daniels, *Concentration Camps U.S.A. Japanese Americans and World War II* (Hinsdale: The Dryden Press, 1971), pp. 85-86.

[15]George C. Dyer, *On the Treadmill to Pearl Harbor: The Memoirs of Admiral James O. Richardson* (Washington D.C. Naval History Division, 1973), pp. 338-39.

[16]Thomas B. Buell, *The Quiet Warrior: A Biography of Admiral Raymond A. Spruance* (Boston: Little Brown and Company, 1974), p. 80.

[17]Letter from Admiral Harold Stark to Admiral James O. Richardson on May 27, 1940, *Pearl harbor Hearings,* Part XIV, p. 2106.

[18]*Ibid.*

[19]*Our Navy,* November 1, 1940, p. 38.

[20]*Long Beach Press-Telegram,* October 14, 1940.

[21]*Ibid.,* October 19, 1940.

[22]*Ibid.,* November 13, 1940.

[23]Arnold S. Lott and Robert F. Sumrall, *Pearl Harbor Attack* (Pompton Lakes: Leeward Publications, 1974), p. 24.

APPENDIX

SHIPS OF THE PACIFIC BATTLE FLEET

Home based in San Pedro in the nineteen thirties.

Battleships:
- Arizona
- Arkansas
- California
- Colorado
- Idaho
- Nevada
- New Mexico
- New York
- Maryland
- Oklahoma
- Mississippi
- Tennessee
- Texas
- West Virginia
- Wyoming
- Pennsylvania

Aircraft Carriers:
- Saratoga
- Lexington

Repair Ships:
- Argonne
- Medusa
- Vestal

Hospital Ships:
- Mercy
- Relief

Compiled by Dick Wolfe.
San Pedro Poet Laureate.

LIST OF BATTLESHIPS HOMEPORTED In San Pedro Bay 1919-40

USS WYOMING (BB-32).......... 1919-20
USS AKANSAS (BB-33).......... 1919-21
USS NEW YORK (BB-34).. 1919, 1926-27
USS TEXAS (BB-35) 1919,1929, 1931-36
USS NEVADA (BB-36).... 1925, 1930-40
USS OKLAHOMA (BB-37) 1921-27,30-40
USS PENNSYLYVANIA (BB-38) . 1922-40
USS ARIZONA (BB-39) 1921-40
USS NEW MEXICO (BB-40) 1919-40
USS MISSISSIPPI (BB-41) 1919-40
USS IDAHO (BB-42)............ 1919-40
USS TENNESSEE (BB-43) 1921-40
USS CALIFORNIA (BB-44) 1921-40
USS COLORADO (BB-45)....... 1924-40
USS MARYLAND (BB-46)....... 1923-40
USS WEST VIRGINIA (BB-48) ... 1924-40

SELECTED BIBLIOGRAPHY

Annual Reports of the Fleets and Task Forces of the U.S. Navy, 1920-1941. Rolls 1-10. Washington D.C.: National Archives and Record Service, General Services Administration, 1974.

Beach, Samuel Wheeler. *The Great Cruise of 1925.* San Francisco: International Printing, 1925.

Buel, Thomas B. *The Quiet Warrior: A Biography of Admiral Raymond A. Spruance.* Boston: Little Brown and Company, 1974.

Hayes, John D. "Admiral Joseph Mason Reeves, USN, Part II, 1931-1948," *Naval War College Review,* January 1977.

Pratt, William V. *Autobiography of William V. Pratt, USN* Washington D.C.: Naval Historical Center, Washington Navy Yard, microfilm, NRS 145, n.d.

Richardson, James O. *On the Treadmill to Pearl Harbor.* Washington D.C.: Navy History Division, 1973.

Stirling, Yates. *Sea Duty: The Memoirs of a Fighting Admiral.* New York: G.P. Putnam's Sons, 1939.

Tuleja, Thaddeus V., *Statesmen and Admirals: Quest for a Far Eastern Naval Policy.* New York: W.W. Norton Inc., 1963.

Wheeler, Gerald E. *Admiral William Veazie Pratt: A Sailor's Life.* Washington D.C.: Naval History Division, 1974.

Wheeler, Gerald E. *Prelude to Pearl Harbor: U.S. Navy and the Far East, 1921-1931.* Columbia: University of Missouri Press, 1963.

Wiley, Henry A. *An Admiral from Texas.* New York: Doubleday, Doran and Company, 1934.

PERIODICALS

LONG BEACH PRESS TELEGRAM
LOS ANGELES TIMES
OUR NAVY MAGAZINE, 1919-1941
SAN PEDRO NEWS PILOT

ABOUT THE AUTHOR

Harvey M. Beigel has taught history for 27 years, the last 24 of which were at Venice High School in Los Angeles, California. During this time, Mr. Beigel also taught at Los Angeles City College. He also has been a consultant for the College Board's Advanced Placement program. His article titled "Pig Boats of San Pedro" was published in *Sea Classics Magazine* in 1982. Soon to be published in *Proceedings of the United States Naval Institute* is his article "San Pedro Long Beach: The American Battle Fleet's Home Port: 1919-1940." He is currently working on an article titled "The Strange Last Cruise of UB-88." He is a member of the San Pedro Bay Historical Society, the Los Angeles Maritime Museum and the Friends of the Cabrillo Marine Museum. He resides with his wife, Elizabeth, in Rancho Palos Verdes, California.